Comments about Manitonquat from gkesedtanamoogk, Wampanoag elder and teacher of Native Studies at the University of Maine:

The work that You have been engaged with over the many years---raising Communities in centered humanity---spirituality---is really at the Heart of the Sacred and the greater promise for the future.

...maintaining a People's History is both a fine art and an evocative response to the incoherence, tyranny, and cynicism of modernity."

"Manitonquat is one of the Wampanoag Nation's leading national treasures."

THE ORIGINAL INSTRUCTIONS

Reflections of an Elder on the Teachings of the Elders, Adapting Ancient Wisdom to the Twenty-First Century

MANITONQUAT (MEDICINE STORY)

authorHOUSE®

AuthorHouse™
1663 Liberty Drive
Bloomington, IN 47403
www.authorhouse.com
Phone: 1-800-839-8640

First published by AuthorHouse   10/7/2009

ISBN: 978-1-4389-8079-9 (sc)

Printed in the United States of America
Bloomington, Indiana

This book is printed on acid-free paper.

Cover art and frontespiece "Turtle Island" by Vincent Nardone

Purpose And Dedication

The idea and motivation for the book you are holding now came as I was speaking as usual of the Original Instructions of Creation to our Native prison circles and to people of my band, the Assonet Wampanoag. As I am getting older the thought is forced on me that almost all the beloved elders from whom I learned when younger, have left us to go on their Star Journey to the Land of Souls. Many of my own generation who were teaching the wisdom of our Old Ways have left us. I see their faces smiling at me, reminding me, "You are our last living link to the world, to the future, the unborn generations. Do not fail us."

One day in the northern-most prison of our state, near the Canadian border, I was speaking, as I often do, about the Original Instructions. An Abenaki member of the circle asked me to write about those Instructions and about the teachings of my elders and what I had learned in my life. He said he had no other elders than me, and reminded me that I am getting old. That was the spur I needed to write this book.

There are many in our prison circles who have no elders, and many in my own band who look to me as elder, asking that I once more take up the pen to record the spiritual teachings they seek in the distressed and confused world of today.

As I have grown older I have begun to understand the great sadness that the elders who spoke to me were carrying because so many of the younger generations were not listening and heeding them as they had their own elders. Too many of our young people, understandably angry, are directed by that anger to fight the non-Indian, but all the great elders of many nations across Turtle Island instructed me not to fight but to teach the non-Indian. I made a solemn commitment to follow their instructions and I have held to it, even though there are a few who have blamed me for that. Therefore, following Slow Turtle's policy, I continue to hold our prison circles open to all who come sincerely to learn how to walk the good red road in a sacred manner.

And so I acknowledge and dedicate this to all those teachers who have gone on, especially to my dear Yetsi Blue, Janet McCloud, Tulalip, and most especially my very dearest and closest partner, friend, and medicine man, Chickatoonapa, Slow Turtle, John Peters, both of whom continue to keep an eye on me from the Spirit World and straighten me out when I need it.

To tell the truth my elders saved me
But handed me too a great heartache
And I feel it deeply now, their heartache
That they could not save their own people

Their concern with me was to keep their truth
And show it only to those coming to seek it
There is a practical wisdom in that, a hope
And a gift that could save the world. Perhaps

For I feel myself inadequate, if only
I could reveal with all the power I felt
From them to the world it would see as I
Have seen, and as I, would then be saved

I don't know if my elders knew how well I heard
Or if others truly listened. Now they have gone
I can only continue to share this truth
Hoping one may listen – could it be you?

CONTENTS

Contents

who had invested so much of himself in this story of darkness and evil that he
could not let it go. He felt betrayed by the others. So he began to play bad tricks
on them all to prove..............................but the people only
laughed and said, "Oh, that's just old Cheepii," and paid him no attention. So

The Story of Cheepii

There are stories about an impish character of our people who used to play bad
tricks on people. My grandfather told one about how he got that way. One of
Creator's helpers, Hobbomokko, came upon this man, Cheepii, and warned him
that Creator was making many mistakes, and because of that there were dark evil
forces at work in the world making it a dangerous place.

Cheepii had not heard such a story before. He thought like this: if the
Creation is a good place and Creator has not made any mistakes, then why did he
make a spirit like Hobbomokko who thinks it is full of evil forces and dangerous?
He asked what he could do, and Hobbomokko told him to collect all the magic
power he could find and make may ceremonies to protect himself.

From that time on Cheepii neglected his family, his house, his canoe, his
garden, and spent all his time searching for power objects – plants, stones, bones,
feathers – and making rituals of protection. At first the people thought that he
was crazy, but they worried lest there be any truth in his story and they began to
neglect their families, their houses, their canoes, their gardens, and spend their
time colleting power objects and making protection rituals.

Soon they began to get sick, as people do when they worry too much. They
went to our first teacher, the spirit being Maushop, to seek healing. When
Maushop saw what was happening he gathered the people in the village.

"Someone told you the Creator has made mistakes and made bad things," he
said, "that is not true. Everything is working just as it should. The plants and the
animals are following their instructions and living in balance. Only some human
beings do not know their instructions and are causing trouble now. Creator allows
all kinds of thinking, but if you follow Hobbomokko's way of thinking you will
disturb the balance and harmony and make trouble for yourselves.

"There are," he said, "three ways in which one can learn the instructions which
allow people to live in balance , in a good way, in beauty and happiness. The first
way is to notice and learn how the Creation works through observation of the
natural world . The second way is to seek inside ourselves, for the Creator also
exists there. The third way is a combination of the first two ways. It is to come
together to learn from each other, and from all those who came before us, all that
has been discovered by observation and meditation. This is the way of ceremony.
Through our stories and our songs and our sharing with each other our wisdom we
increase our knowledge and pass it on to the coming generations.

So the people returned with a new understanding of the uses of observation,
meditation and ceremony, and they grew strong again. Except for poor Cheepii,

who had invested so much of himself in this story of darkness and evil that he could not let it go. He felt betrayed by the others. So he began to pay bad tricks on them all, to prove there really was evil in the world. But the people only laughed and said, "Oh, that's just old Cheepii" and paid him no attention. So eventually he just packed up and left, and no one knew where he went.

But some of us figure that he must have found other people who believed in his story, because about four hundred years ago we started getting all these boat people from over the sea who were all dressed in black and talking about Sin, Damnation, and the Devil!

PROLOGUE
Discovering the True Human Being

Come in, come in. Have a seat anywhere -pick any chair - I'll take your coat. There's tea and coffee and cakes on the table. Settle back a bit and just take in the scene through our big French doors there. Such a beautiful winter morning here in our New Hampshire woods. The sun is brilliant on the snow, and the sky is a rich blue above the playful tops of the birch trees. The titmouse, the nuthatch, and the chickadees are vying for our sunflower seeds with a red and two gray squirrels.

Before we begin, let us take a moment to get here, to this moment in our lives. First, consider where you are on your journey through your life. What has happened to bring you to this place and this moment, to make your heart and mind what it is now?

And then let us open our hearts and minds further, expand our circle to include not only what we see here, but all that is going on on this small ball we call the Earth. See it in your mind now, as the astronauts do, as a tiny blue dot. What is its story, and how did that affect us and bring us to where we are now? What is happening at this moment all over this world? To the people of this continent, to the people in all the other continents, to the animal and plant relatives that share this world with us. Now, none of us know what will happen in the story of this world. But it is clear that its future is very much in our own hands. It is human beings that have put it in jeopardy and only human beings that can save it. Only human beings. Only me. Only you. We should consider this closely, and learn everything we can about our responsibilities here.

So I'm glad you came. Because there are things I am supposed to tell you, to inform you - to inform anyone who wants to listen. A long time ago I began to hear these things from my elders, from many elders in many of the First Nations of Turtle Island - North America. As they shared the instructions they had received from their elders when they were young they told us we must share them with others as well.

I am supposed to convey a very important message to you.

Important? Yes, this message was of great importance to the elders from whom I first heard it, and now it is important to me. And I believe it to be of the greatest importance to you as well, to the survival of our species and the continuation of evolution. So more than important: imperative. And urgent.

Let me begin by explaining how I came to be in this position. I am not alone in this, and it is not my idea. There are many messengers at this time who are engaged in a life's work of transmitting to the world the ancient teaching of our Native elders. I am not unique at all, except that the way I shall relate this story must be different according to my own individual path and history. Therefore I would like to tell my story very briefly first, that you may understand why and how I came to this work.

Fifty years ago I was a writer, trying to discover what was wrong with human beings and how we might help ourselves. But the more I studied in philosophy, psychology, history, sociology and religion, the more I saw that what I sought was not to be found in books. Yet I felt that knowledge must somewhere exist. I wished that my Wampanoag grandfather Wuninam, who had taught me so much when I was a boy, was still alive. I spoke to other elders among our people, wise and good people, but when I asked why human beings were so crazy, violent and destructive, they were as much in the dark as I was.

In the 1950s and 60s I had an exciting life as a playwright and director of my own devoted little theatre group of dedicated and quite brilliant performers and artists in New York City. It was very fulfilling for me, engaging all my creativity with freedom to explore whatever my mind could conceive. But in the sixties I began to undergo what I can only call a spiritual crisis. The government escalated its interference in Vietnam for commercial and political reasons into a war. Crime, violence, and drugs moved into our neighborhood. Repressive force was used against protestors of the war, civil rights abuse and the dangers of nuclear power. In a year and a half four colleagues of mine in the theatre killed themselves. I thought, what is going on?

I knew I had nothing useful to bring to these problems through my art, because I did not understand the underlying causes. I studied social and political thinkers, psychological and religious thinkers, philosophy and history, ancient and modern, western and eastern.

I did learn a lot in that period, but nothing to explain why humankind had gone so far wrong. Nothing to give me hope that we could transform a destructive, toxic civilization into a stable, peaceful, healthy society. Yet somehow I felt there might be a knowledge somewhere that contained the essential wisdom for humanity.

I left my beloved theatre company. I left all the world I knew and set out to seek and to learn, asking, listening. Finding from many a little something useful for the journey. But not the answer I sought: how did humankind, once promising so much, get to the disastrous condition of today's world that bids fair to destroy itself? So I left our homelands and went west to see what I could learn. I got involved in liberating political actions, in transcendental mystical experiences, adventures in conscioiusness, and in the discoveries of humanistic psychology and wholistic health. But I found only partial cures to a few limited symptoms. It was not until I journeyed to find the native elders and spiritual leaders of the other First Nations that I found the complete answer that made me understand. I began to find elders further removed from the dominant culture, still in touch with ancient knowledge passed through oral traditions of ceremony, song and story.

Most of these elders were not educated in dominant culture schools beyond fifth grade. Some neither wrote nor read. Some spoke little or no English and had to be translated. But it was from them I learned the knowledge that made what was happening understandable, and the wisdom to see the way out of humanity's dilemma.

Human Beings Had Forgotten their Instructions

I traveled all over North America listening to these elders. They each had different images, stories and prophecies, but the message was similar everywhere. When I asked these elders why human beings were doing such terrible things to the earth and each other, they told me that human beings had forgotten their instructions. That was something I had not heard before, and I listened carefully.

Everything in Creation, they said, has a spirit that is instructed by the Source of Being, the Spirit of Creation. And therefore all is equal, and all is sacred. What this means, they would say, is that the Creation is good and perfect in every way. It functions reliably and well, is in every way beautiful.

Through the Spirit of Creation all spirits are related. Each functions and fulfills itself following its natural law, known to many Native people as the Original Instructions. These are the instructions that make the grass grass and be green or yellow or brown, that make the apple tree blossom and make apples and not acorns or pine nuts, that make the geese fly south in winter while crow and blue jay watch them but stay behind. The sun follows instructions to bestow energy, warmth and light, the moon travels dependably to show phases by which one can mark time's passing, the earth follows the path that brings the renewing of the seasons in a circle.

This is not to say it was all placed here for us, that human beings are the reason and ultimate intention of this Creation. It is a mystery that the wisest philosophers and scientists do not have the answer to. If you believe you understand the mystery and know its secret, I will respect your belief.

Life grows, reproduces, and declines, eating and being eaten, transformed to new life. It all functions immaculately. There is a balance and a harmony to it all. To sit on a hill apart from human beings you may be able to feel all this. The balance, the harmony, the interconnectedness, the completeness, the perfection of all Creation. Then it may come to you that you are not an outside observer. You are one with all Creation, a relative to all that is. Therefore you have a place and a function, and you also are complete and perfect. Sacred.

Then you go down from the hill where you felt the inner depths of Reality, everything following its instructions in balance and harmony and all working well. You get into your automobile, exuding poisons into the air, and meet thousands of your kind spreading their poisons on the highways as you head into the smoggy, noisy city where the human beings are stressed, confused, lonely, unhappy, angry and increasingly violent.

What has happened?

The old ones shake their heads sadly. It's quite clear to all of them. The human beings have forgotten their instructions. They must have known them at one time, as all creatures do, but somehow their ancestors misplaced them, or set them aside, no longer realizing their importance.

People without their Original Instructions are people without the guidance of the spirit. They do not know their true natures, nor their true place and function in Creation. Most of them have no belief or even knowledge of the spirit and try to content themselves with acquisitions of material things, of power and prestige among other human beings. Others, with a growing sense of spiritual emptiness, seek to fill that void through the scriptures, books, rituals and disciplines devised by various human cultures over the centuries.

Everyone takes what his culture gives and figures out how to survive. But survival is not enough, and now our cultures threaten even that.

When I had been absorbing the knowledge and wisdom of the elders for some time I began to understand there was something I was to do with this learning. At the same time some non-Indian people were asking that I come and speak with them about the old ways. I asked the elders I was close to then if they thought I should. They said they felt that Creation had given me this journey for a reason. They said there was a reason why I was born half Indian and half European-American, and why I had been given a western university education. I had read the stories of the dominant culture, understood their thinking, but my grandfather's stories had led me back to the path of Creation, to learn the Original Instructions. And I had learned to speak and write clearly in the English language. From all that it was quite clear to them that it was my function to communicate the essential knowledge of the Original Instructions to the world beyond.

They cautioned me not to act like the missionaries, not to accost those who did not care to listen, but only to bring my story and their knowledge to those who are seeking it and ask me for it. Since that time, instructed by all these elders whom I consulted, I have gone only where I have been invited, and spoken only to those who have invited me.

Even the books I have written, five before this one, were devised only at the request of other people for the specific knowledge in each one. The first two books of lore and stories of our people were requested by various elders, teachers and friends among our Wampanoag and other north-eastern peoples as we talked together at ceremonies about the old ways. The third book was written at the request of prisoners and others who wanted to know more of our native prison circles, and the fourth at the request of members of a distant circle who wanted to know more about the making and functioning of a circle, the fifth by students eager to change society.

Since then I have spoken to many thousands of people over the years, but there still is much I have learned that I have not yet shared fully. And people keep reminding me that I am getting along in years, that I had better speak out while I can. Though I have seen eighty winters now I don't feel very different in my body, and so I am shocked when I accidentally catch a glimpse of some strange old man smiling at me from a mirror!

The impetus for this book also comes from the request of some of our prisoners. One day, in one of our circles, I told the prisoners I had some sense of urgency to impart to them the knowledge I had received from my elders. All but one of those elders have left us now, I told them, and I myself am growing old. If I do not succeed to pass along what I have been given in my life, then the gift will have been in vain, and the knowledge will be buried with me.

This was of course overly dramatic for my point, because there are many others conveying similar knowledge, but I hoped it would make them listen carefully and learn. These prisoners come mainly from backgrounds that gave them little support. Many were adopted, or raised in institutions, or had dysfunctional, violent, alcoholic families. No elders, no community, no one to provide guidance and spiritual understanding. For most in that circle I and a few other elders who have visited them are their only guide to our spiritual heritage. And so some of them pleaded that I set down in a book all I could remember of our Original Instructions.

And so, my grandchildren, here is your book.

It should be emphasized that our people had no scriptures and no body of accepted orthodoxy. There were many cultures with very different ceremonies and stories. The notion of Original Instructions was not expressed in that way in all cultures, central in many, but considered in some detail in but few. But the elders refer to human values often. What follows is the product of both my memory and my meditation. It is not to be memorized as catechism, but only thought upon.

The Original Instructions were not written by any of our holy people or prophets. The Creator did not hand us numbered proscriptions on tablets of stone. The Original Instructions are to be found only in the book of nature. They have been interpreted, verified, and passed on to us by generations of our ancestors in oral traditions. So of course they do not exist in twelve chapters as I have set them down here for clarity and simplicity. You cannot speak of the twelve Original Instructions, because the number of instructions are as infinite as Creation. But most of the elders emphasize certain ones, and I have selected those that I feel are of exceptional importance for human beings today. I have taken my arbitrary selection of twelve instructions and arranged them in groups of three to make four parts. Perhaps because traditional Native thought tends to be in fours, and so I have corresponded these four parts to four directions of a medicine wheel.

Things to Think About

What I write today is a combination of what I have remembered of the teachings I have heard from elders with what I have read myself in the book of nature and in that book within myself. At the end of each chapter I have added a paragraph of "things to think about" that might be interesting to those who teach or discuss these writings in a goup, and something in verse to give another slant on the subject. I suggest you do not read the whole book at once. Only take in one chapter a day and think about it. If you have a class or a circle it would be good to use the "things to think about" for discussion.

The truth of Creation is within you, within us all. Let therefore your own spirit debate or confirm or expand these messages passed to us by the elders, thought upon and verified by centuries even millennia of human experience. I have thought quite a bit about the responsibility of passing on the wisdom of the elders. To the youth of my own people, to those in the circles of the prisons, and to seeking human beings everywhere. Most of the elders who passed on their knowledge to us, and all of the wisest and most large-minded, in my opinion, always believed the knowledge was for all people. It was not Indian ways, they often said, but human being ways that they spoke of. The Original Instructions, which were given to all humankind.

Some of what I want to talk about will be new to you, and some of it you will know already, just as some of what the elders revealed long ago was familiar to me. But I needed and we all need to be reminded of these things again and again as we struggle with our lives. I hope and believe you will find revelations as I did that will make your journey clearer, with greater meaning and purpose.

More than ever in these times, it seems to me, we all need to think upon these Original Instructions of how to be a true human being.

PART ONE

DIRECTION NORTH – Ground of our Being

ELEMENT EARTH

The three basic instructions for the human
species to survive, live well,
and contribute to the web of life on earth
in a good way, in other words,

HOW TO BE A REAL HUMAN BEING
AND WALK IN A SACRED MANNER

1. RESPECT

2. THE CIRCLE: RELATIONSHIP

3. THANKSGIVING

PART ONE – NORTH

It is somewhat after the middle of the night now. An unusual time to begin, you may be thinking, but thank you for coming. The time feels right to me. It is the Winter Solstice, the beginning of the end of the old year for most people who follow the ancient ways in the north. Since we are here in the North Country winter will blow some snow and ice our way, but we know that the wheel is turning, spring is coming, sleeping in the ground beneath our feet.

So here we are together in the territory of our relatives, the Wabanaki. I decided for our journeys together here we would not visit the same places we went for the talks of my first book, <u>Return to Creation.</u> I like to ground our talks in an actual locale on the earth to have practical reminders around us and not get too abstract. When we separate ourselves from the natural environment we tend to get a bit unreal. True patriotism resides not in love of a flag or a history, but in a love of the land and all the creatures that live and grow there. And one of the most important of all of our Original Instructions I have not elaborated on in this book is the instruction to care for the land and our fellow creatures, which I believe requires us to spend more time in and attention to the natural world that is still preserved and untouched by human hands..

I decided also to start only from places that I know well, where I feel their various spirits deeply, but this time not necessarily from the traditional lands of my own people. We are fortunate to have still a wealth of wild natural places where we can draw deep connection and inspiration. I can draw such inspiration only in memory of having been to and been moved by, for instance, such places as Acadia Nation Park at sunrise, or the great redwoods of California, where coming out of my tent in early morning was like walking into the greatest cathedral on earth, the thin rays of sun falling from on high through the dim hush to the forest floor. Riding my horse reverently over the Great Smokey Mountains or poling a bateau through dim cypress swamps, walking the sands of a small island in the Florida keys, or in awe through the lush rain forests of the Olympic Peninsula, or past the giant saguaro cacti raising their arms as in prayer at sunset in the Sonora Desert.

So I have picked places where I have stood and marveled in each of the four directions from our people's land, places that are emblazoned in my memory, that I carry with me and can return to whenever I choose. I could have chosen to begin in the country of our relatives, the Passamaquoddy, as their lands are the furthest east of any in the United States, or we might have gone up to Cape Breton Island, even further east, where our supreme sachem Drifting Goose retired among our MicMac relatives. But I decided to begin here on Mt. Desert Island because of the mountain. This is a very special mountain, with a strong spirit that calls to me, a very sacred spot where I have experienced healing and learning when I was young, and I am hoping it may again guide my thoughts to convey to you some of the most important lessons I have learned in almost eight decades of living and adventuring on this wondrous Earth, our home.

This mountain used to be known as Green Mountain, I suppose for all the evergreens it raises toward the sky, but in the last century it got renamed Mount Cadillac for that extravagant and grandiose French adventurer and poseur who also liked to rename himself. It is brisk and chilly up here so bundle up, and we'll gather close to the little fire we have kindled. This is the highest point on the eastern edge of Turtle Island, known today as North America. This is Wapanak country, a federation of nations in northern New England and maritime Canada, part of a larger northeastern Algonquin family that includes my people, the Wampanoag, who live south of here, on the southeast coast of Massachusetts and Rhode Island.

I like to start from a prospect looking down on land and sea, among the winds and clouds, nearer the stars. And though it is north of our lands it is also very far to the east from us. I like to begin ceremonies looking toward the North, a very old custom, and I also like beginning with the vernal equinox, as that is the beginning time of the year for most people, and that spring season we associate with the East. So here we are, coming from winter into spring, from North to East.

Let us join our hands at this time and feel our connection in this circle. Let us look into each other's eyes and give thanks that we are together at this time. Then, as our people like to begin, let us bring our hearts and minds together and with one intention give our greetings to our Mother Earth.

As we do that we recall that everything we need is provided by her to care for us every day, and whatever we may have, including our very bodies, is a gift from this beautiful and generous mother. Some day our bodies will wear out, and we will return them to her to be recycled into other life. But until then she will continue to provide for us as long as we protect and care for her. So let us with one heart and one mind give our thanksgiving to Mother Earth.

Next, she will be very happy if we remember to greet all of her children, the family of which we are a part. We greet the plant people that put down their roots into the Earth, and recall all their gifts of food and shelter and fuel and medicine. We greet the animal people who dig into the earth, crawl and run and fly and swim, and recall all the many gifts and the lessons they give us. And we greet all the other human people who struggle all over the Earth and often share what they have and what they know with us. So we put our hearts and minds together to send our thanksgiving to all our relatives all over the Earth.

And then we look up and see all those tiny lights blinking in the vast dark over our heads. We are told they are really great fires like our Grandfather Sun, only very far away. We are told they are only the very closest stars in a spiraling island of millions, billions of them, that beyond them in dark oceans of space are millions more such islands unimaginably distant from us and from each other.

Grandfather Sun and Grandmother Moon just now are on the other side of our Earth, the one bestowing energy and light to us and the other reflecting them. The moon in her changing brings cycles of cleansing and fertility and shows us when to plant the seeds that the sun and rain will cause to grow. We do not know if other beings inhabit other worlds out there, but a there are so many it may be so. Contemplating all of that makes us understand how tiny is this spinning pebble we call the Earth, but we know that everything out there follows the same instructions, that we are all playing a part in the same story, which has one beginning, a common journey through time, and presumably one end. We are given so much and learn so much from all these distant relatives that we want now to send them our thanksgiving with one heart and mind.

When we have thought of all there is that we know of, and all we do not know, and all we may have forgotten, there remains one thing beyond. And that is the Source of all of it. We cannot find anything here that is capable of conceiving and manifesting such a Creation. It has a beginning, but what was there before that? We do not know. This Creation is so vast and complex it confounds our ability to comprehend it.

It is impossible for us to imagine what caused this Creation. But we do not doubt that we exist and that this Earth and this universe exist, so we go on trying to imagine what is impossible to imagine. We even give this Source names, such as God, Allah, Kiehtan, but these are only noises we fashion to be able to refer to what we don't understand, noises that may give us comfort if we make them often, if we sing of them. Strangest of all is that we then argue with each other about the nature and the stories of this Source that is unknown. In our short history we have convinced ourselves that only our stories are true and we have often fought, killed, and died to convince others that we know better than they. Well, I certainly don't want to start any fights right here at the beginning of our explorations together, so let's just agree about one thing: we are alive. We are living here together in this time, and that is wonderful. A miracle, if you will, that must give us all great joy. It will make us feel even better to give our gratitude for this miracle to that Source, whatever we may call it or however we conceive it. So at this time we can with one heart and one mind send our thanksgiving to that great Mystery, the Creator.

You see why this is such a good way to begin together. We are reminded of essential realities we don't often think about. We get so pre-occupied with our little selves and our little problems, our brief time here, we don't notice how small

5

they are and how vast is the universe and its amazing progress through time. We don't think all that out there has anything to do with us. But it *is* us. We forget that we are family, that we are related not only to each other but to all that is.

It is in that perspective of time that we can rejoice in the gathering of star stuff that gave birth to this planet, and in the coming together of just the right elements and conditions to bring forth life, and in the evolutionary instructions that gave rise to the little tribes of our ancestors that wandered forth to find their homes across the Earth.

I want to speak to you of what I was taught by my elders, coming in a long line from those ancestors, of what they learned that proved useful, and what should be discarded. Those elders told me that the instructions deep inside me had brought me to them, and that I was supposed to pass on the instructions, not only to my own people, my family and my nation, but also to all people and all nations, to anyone who seeks them. Now all those elders and teachers have passed from the flow of this life, and I am myself an elder, an old man carrying the teachings that have been passed through generations, adding some knowledge gained in the specific happenings of my own days.

It is time for me now, while I am alive and still able, to pass on what I know. In these talks through the year to come I will try to concentrate on what I feel are the most important instructions for this time we are sharing. And now that I write them down you will be able to keep them and go back to them when you wish. Because some of these instructions will seem more important and useful to you one time, and another time others may speak more meaningfully to you. It is my hope that this may be a small link, however incomplete and inadequate, between you and my beloved elders.

Here below the dark vault above us, there to the north, the east and the south, lie the dark unseen waters that embrace all the lands, licking the shores of Nova Scotia, Labrador, Greenland, Iceland, the British Isles, Europe, Africa, Asia, Australia, the islands of the Pacific, South America, and Antarctica. Even as we stand in the cold wind of the mountain the Earth is slowly warming beneath us. In the north and south and across the high mountain ranges the ice has begun to melt. The great glaciers that have stood for millennia are dissolving, new rivers are flowing, and the seas have begun to rise. Before we can stop this many places of human habitation will begin to flood and disappear and many places will dry and cease to provide food and water for animals and people. We must begin to prepare ourselves now to find ways to keep millions of lives from dying of starvation and thirst in India, China, and South America.

It is our species, humankind, that is doing this vast damage. Humankind, the crown of Creation, homo sapiens sapiens, the wise, wise people, the creatures of great heart and sensitivity, the creatures of kindness and compassion, of wondrous creativity and scientific ability, the ones who can love so deeply and experience bliss, joy, ecstasy. It is this species that plunders everything, robs, rapes, pillages and murders its own and every other species, becoming madder, more enraged and more insane with every passing year of its existence.

When I asked my elders many years ago why this was so, they shook their heads sadly.

"People have lost their instructions," they said.

That really woke me up. Instructions? People have instructions? Well, of course we have cultural instructions, we were taught the commandments of our religions, the golden rule, social mores and the laws of the land, but inherent, built-in instructions from the Creation about how to behave?

"Sure," the elders said, "Every thing has its instructions. Look at that grass. It knows how to grow just like that, how tall to be, how green. It doesn't try to be a pine tree. That apple tree doesn't try to grow cherries; it just keeps on appling because that's its instructions. That beaver knows all about cutting trees and building dams and doesn't want to go run with the wolves. That finch just likes to sing in the sun, but that owl waits for dusk to start his hunt in silence. Creation taught them their instructions and they follow them. The mouse takes care of his mouse business and doesn't long to be a rabbit; the eagle, the hawk and the buzzard share the same sky and don't decide to go south with the geese in the fall. Even the waters, the brooks and rivers, the lakes, the sea and the tides, follow their instructions, as do the winds, the thunders and the rain. So do also the Earth, the moon, the sun and all the star nations.

"Only man is confused and does not follow his instructions. So now he is a problem to himself and to all life on Earth."

Now we learn that everything changes. All is changing and developing from the beginning. Slowly, in harmony with all Creation. Once there were monsters, dinosaurs, but they got too big for the environment. The strawberry, the sugar maple, the corn, beans and squash have been developing slowly, and I guess they will continue unless we interfere with them. We have gotten in trouble, though. Changing too fast, without the slow development of evolution.

We learn that humankind developed slowly too. From little weak two-leggeds, over several million years. And for all those time it grew and changed in harmony with everything else. Like a baby it developed, happy and content, learning, playing, and making things, surviving together. Together in their small bands they could explore and care for each other and pass on their knowledge from generation to generation.

Maybe four million years since the first ones we call hominids stood up on their hind legs on the Earth. A long time. Content with each other. In harmony, in balance. Developing their minds, learning communication, cooperating. Creating language to communicate better and better skills not only to survive but also to lead good and happy lives together.

How do I know that? Many ways.

I learn a lot from the stories of our people. Much wisdom about how people lived and learned is contained in stories. The truth of stories is not the material facts but the truth they speak to our inner understanding. We have instructions in our blood, our genes, our cells, our DNA. Many stories tell of long ago times, before history, when people lived together in a good way, when they walked a good red road in a sacred manner, when animals and human beings communicated and agreed to live in harmony and mutual respect, when the plant people revealed their medicines in dreams. Most of the world's cultures have a story about an ancient "golden age" when people lived well without material wealth, simply, with no toil or stress, working together, sharing what they had with each other, caring for the ones who could not work, the sick, the very old and the very young. Their joy was not in possession or status or power, but in each other, in the warmth and closeness of their hearts, in humor and laughter, the stories of the old ones, and the play and growing of the children, doing the task at hand well and carefully, in the beauty of the earth in all weather and all seasons.

As old Nick Black Elk said, we were once a strong and happy people, and so I believe were all peoples once, living in a circle and guided by the Original Instructions.

1. RESPECT

Wherever you may travel throughout North America you will hear one instruction given first and foremost by all the Indians to their children and to those seekers from other lands. That instruction is Respect.

The first instruction must be respect. Because whatever else our relationship could be, if we don't respect our home, this planet earth and all its processes, we are contributing to the diminution and destruction of all life here, including our own.

Whatever human beings have not created they must respect.

We did not create this universe and everything in it, the stars, the Earth, life, and the laws, the instructions that govern them. Some other power has caused all this to be. It is beyond our understanding. It is beyond the understanding of the scientists and the philosophers and the priests, it is beyond the understanding of Buddha, Moses, Jesus, and all the scriptures - no matter what they may say or believe.

We do not know why the Creation exists. All we know is that it exists, it is really there, we are really here, so we must respect it all or we will surely destroy it.

Whatever we have not created must be respected.

We did not create this beautiful earth that bore and supports us.

She gifts us with all we require for life. Every day she provides us with food and fuel and shelter and medicine. She is a bountiful and generous mother and has everywhere holy places that heal us and revive our spirits. It is too bad for us when we separate ourselves from her, too bad because then we miss one of the deepest joys in life.

We did not create life. We may learn how to replicate it in our laboratories, but that would be imitation, not creation. The simplest leaf is a marvel and a mystery and a universe to contemplate. Every plant that sets its roots and clings to Mother Earth for life is a miracle beyond comprehension. Even if we are blind to their beauty and splendor, we must respect that life. When we do not, we allow the extermination of beings that provide us with oxygen, food, fuel, shelter, clothing, and medicine.

We did not create the animals, our companions here on this journey through life. From the simplest one-celled beings to the great blue whales, to the complexity of the thinking human creature, each life has a place in the great harmony, in the on-going process of Creation. Because of our arrogance and our disrespect, we human beings are driving thousands of species of plant and animal life to extinction every year. Our supposedly informed leaders cannot agree to preserve them. I wonder did they all miss that biology class where we learned that the strength of life is in its diversity?

We did not create the moon that lovingly circles us above. Now that human beings have learned how to travel there they even begin to think of ways to exploit this beauty we call our grandmother, to steal from her and build factories and tourist hotels and generally trash her as we are now trashing our beautiful Earth. The Hopi people warn us from their prophecies that if we do not respect the moon and leave her as she is there will be dire consequences for our human society.

We did not create the sun, that star that provides all our light and energy, that makes it just warm enough to support life, not too hot and not too cold. Think how dangerous it is to tamper with that very precise balance. Think now that for the first time in the history of life on this planet a developing species, Homo sapiens, has begun to disturb that relationship. We have blown open continually expanding holes in the protective ozone layer and the full force of the sun's radiation is being loosed upon many areas. We have covered the planet with a canopy of pollution that the sun's penetrating rays are beginning to cook and melt our glaciers and disturb our weather patterns. No one can now predict the ultimate outcome of this ignorance and disrespect.

We did not create all the beings that revolve in the great circle of the universe. If I were an intelligent life form from another planet that had learned to live in harmony and respect, following Creation's instructions, and I were able to observe the antics of human beings on planet earth, I would be deeply concerned for our universe. I would understand that we all are relatives, and that what any member of our family does without respect has an unpredictable effect on the entire web of Creation.

We did not create the Creator of all that, and we did not create ourselves. When we listen only to ourselves, pay attention only to our selfish and temporary desires, when we do not consider and respect the purposes of Creation, we become ungrateful recipients of the greatest gifts, selfishly taking all with no thought of the giver or the reason for the gifts. When we do not consider the whole of which we are but a part, we become a renegade and outlaw species. We become a cancer slowly eating away the essence of existence.

Respect is the primary instruction because it is the very minimum required of us to survive and not to interfere with the harmony of existence and the purposes and processes of Creation.

It is because all of Creation is sacred and holy that we respect it. All of it. Every part, with no exception.

This is a time when many old religions are fading away and being abandoned. Also many are being renewed and reborn with new understanding. And at this time many others try to fashion new religions eclectically borrowing and melding what still holds inspiration from all the world's spiritual traditions. It seems to me very sad that the modern reaction against much of organized religion has left us today with very little sense or belief in the sacred and the holy.

But there is a need in human beings for spiritual understanding. Many more people, more and more in this age, have decided against any tradition, any religion, any set of scriptures or stories. They no longer struggle to find meaning in ancient teachings. Still the longing is there. Not to be cut off from the process of Creation, not to be isolated and abandoned to our very limited human knowledge. They may not realize it, but most people seem to be searching for that lost sense of the sacred and the holy.

There is a tradition we have for people with such a longing to go away from the man-made world for a time. Leaving human society and all its connections and admonitions. Leaving family and friends, teachers and studies, work and ambition, leaving all roles, all stress, to be alone in the purely natural world. Making a place there, on a hill or a mountain or a dune, in a wood, a meadow or a desert. Setting aside time from our engagement in human society, a few days and nights, or a week, even a month, at the very least a full night and a day.

At first we may feel like an observer in that place, a visitor, a stranger in this world. When we really get to know it we begin to feel at home there. We understand that we belong. We are related to all this, to everything in Creation.

We see then that the Creation is one great web. All is in relationship, and it all works together. It functions elegantly. It fits. Everything in this web has its part. Everything is equal and important to the whole. This is part of what we mean when we say everything is sacred and holy. The design of existence is far beyond our meager human capabilities to understand and comprehend. Anything we diminish or destroy disturbs the whole in ways we cannot predict.

Since you and I are equal parts of this web, equally important and equally necessary to the whole, it follows we are also equally sacred and holy and deserving of respect.

In the prisons I meet men raised in institutions, foster homes, dysfunctional families, and on the streets. What they have learned is that respect must be earned, most often by physical force and violence. I tell them that in our circles they don't need to earn respect. They deserve respect because they are children of the Creator of all, and are therefore sacred and holy. I tell them our first instruction is respect, and the elders have told us that this must be the center of all our circles.

I tell them that respect is not like love. Respect must come first, before love. People do not will or control with their minds whom or what they will love. I

11

cannot insist that you love anyone. Jesus exhorted people to love one another, to love even their enemies, and that was a great concept. But in two thousand years only a very few people have managed to do that. Even people today calling themselves Christians don't seem to be able to love their enemies. But respect is something you can choose. You can decide and will yourself to respect anyone and anything.

The prisoners understand this quickly. They make that agreement and remind each other when they slip and forget. They keep the respect strong in their circles when elders are present. If elders do not get to the prison for a while, in that disrespectful and demoralizing environment they may forget sometimes, and then they see the circle does not work for them when respect is not honored.

It is so apparent in the prison circles, the absolute necessity that respect be the primary and central concern, the foundation of the circle, and thence of all relationships. Because respect was never accorded them and was unknown in their experience of growing up they know how easy it is to forget and for old patterns to dictate their behavior. So they understand that they must keep reminding each other and reminding themselves about the primacy and necessity of respect.

The prison circles are a good model to help the rest of the world to understand the importance of this first instruction. The societies of earth have lost the Original Instructions, and respect is not taught to the children of earth. It is often demanded, but that is not the way to teach. The way to teach respect, of course, is to show it and give it.

For instance, take your own experience. In your childhood how many people respected you completely? Who was it, when you were a young person, who treated you with absolute respect, who accepted you completely, who appreciated your qualities and helped you, by their admiration, to admire and appreciate yourself?

Probably not many, if any.

When we are young we do not see many examples of people respecting each other. Elders are not respected in the dominant cultures of the west. They are ignored, pushed aside, sometimes abused, objects of humor and derision, at best only tolerated. Poor people are not respected by those who are well-off, people of color are not respected by the police, young people are given no respect anywhere, the earth and its plant and animal life get little thought or respect, and so on. The only thing that can be seen to be afforded respect is material wealth. So the moral message of this society is only that you must get rich, however you may do it, and then you will be sure to get respect.

What if all human beings were brought up believing the earth is precious, that every part of it is sacred and holy? What if we saw, from birth, everyone around us being careful and respectful of the natural world, including the plants and animals?

12

What if we ourselves were respected as children by all adults and taught to respect ourselves? It seems to me as though that simple teaching of the first Original Instruction would have a profound impact on our lives and relationships, how we treat ourselves, as well as our fellows and everything outside ourselves.

Have you ever thought about the sacred? Does that word or concept carry any meaning for you?" Is there anything of which you might say "don't mess with that - that is sacred to me?" If nothing is sacred to you, do you think that is a good thing? Would you not rather that every person and every institution consider your life sacred? Would you not rather that they consider your family sacred, you partner, children, parents, your relatives? Would you not rather people consider your home a sacred space, and your right to live unmolested, to live freely without harming others, a sacred right?

You do not have to believe in a Creator or any holy spirit in order to desire to live and to be treated by others in a sacred manner. I believe that the only people who would not desire this are those who have been so badly hurt and damaged that they must require a lot of very deep healing. (That is a valuable work which yet can be accomplished with sufficient attention and time.) But most people in this sad, violent, crazy, often terrifying world really would want to live in a good way, to be respected and treated well by others. To have peace and security and freedom for themselves and their families. If they thought it was possible.

It is possible. It is completely possible for us to live with each other and with the natural world in peace and harmony, balanced, relaxed, and in good health. All it would take is a universal agreement among human beings. An agreement to honor the first instruction of respect.

Whatever is in Creation is necessary and should be respected.

It is necessary because it is here. It exists. With our tiny minds and limited understanding we cannot say the Creation is wrong because it contains things we don't care for, like mosquitoes or bacteria or whatever gives us trouble. Because we also must survive we can give attention to how we can either live together with them or separate them from us, and this can be done with full respect for their being. As we may respect the plants and animals that we consume as food or medicine. We are careful. We pay attention, and give them our respect.

It follows then that you are necessary and should therefore be respected. The concept of respect for others and for the rest of Creation is understandable to most people, but I find that what most of us ignore and neglect is respect for ourselves. Just ask yourself now, do you truly deeply respect yourself? If not, why not? That is a question worth delving into.

Creation has sent you here, into this life, and like everything else you have a reason to be here. Your mind, your awareness may not yet have discovered that purpose, but it is in your being nevertheless. In your instructions. If you do not respect yourself you probably won't find that purpose. If you do not respect yourself you will not be able to fulfill yourself. You will get distracted. Perhaps abuse yourself, mistreat your body, neglect your mind. You may well allow yourself to get stuck in patterns that have no meaning, no joy, no wonder, no purpose but bare survival. Killing time.

Respecting ourselves means giving ourselves good attention. Paying attention to our bodies, our health, what we eat, our physical activity and rest. Paying attention to our minds, to learning and planning and creating. Paying attention to our feelings, being aware, not afraid to feel uncomfortable feelings but not holding on to them, releasing them, letting them go. Celebrating the good feelings, beauty, joy, and love. Respecting ourselves means understanding we are more than our sensations, our thoughts and feelings. We may not know exactly what that "more" is, even if we give it a name, such as "soul" or "spirit". But when we respect ourselves and pay attention we may become aware of something in us that is connected to something infinite and eternal.

When we truly respect ourselves and pay good attention we get to know ourselves. As we get to know ourselves more fully we get to understand ourselves. And as we begin to understand ourselves we begin to like ourselves. We get closer to our real selves. Then, because it is our nature, we start to love ourselves.

It is often said that we cannot truly love others unless we love ourselves. And as we have seen that must begin with respect. We cannot will ourselves to love, even ourselves. But we can decide to respect ourselves. That means giving thoughtful, supportive attention to ourselves, which then leads to understanding, then liking, finally loving.

Probably you have noticed people who seem immediately loveable. Just about everyone loves these people. Why? They are friendly, they are kind, they are sympathetic, they seem to enjoy you and everyone. They are relaxed. They are enjoying themselves. Clearly they respect the sacred gifts they were given, their bodies, their minds and hearts. They are content with themselves and so can be genuinely interested in others.

When these people first meet someone of course it would not be possible for them to like him, not until they know something about him. But their attitude is one of respect, and of paying attention, of openness and a desire to learn about him. When someone approaches us with respect, with attention and openness to learn of us, we are apt to say we really like that person.

I have a friend in England, Scilla Elworthy, who founded the Oxford Research Group to reduce and eliminate nuclear weapons in the world. A world class expert on peace, winner of the Niwana Peace Prize and nominated three times for the Nobel Peace Prize, she gets to speak with defense ministers and foreign minister and heads of state around the world. She treats them respectfully and listens and pays attention to their concerns. Because of that they also respect her, and many seek her counsel in developing their policies.

She is also a founder and director of Peace Direct, an organization seeking to engage individuals in the work of peace on Earth. One of the principal values of this organization is respect. In many books, articles, and speeches she has expounded this theme. "Show respect. A constant theme of my and my colleagues' research has been that humiliation emerges as a key driver of political violence. Conversely, to redress and reduce violence requires systematic training for soldiers and all those involved in conflict in the necessessityfor respect for other cultures. This means in the training of police and armed forces, not only knowledge of customs and religious sensitivities, but also education in awareness – understanding why respect is so important.....If someone feels deeply insulted by another he is hardly likely to behave in a peaceful and cooperative way, whereas if the other speaks in a respectful, non-aggressive manner – even if there is profound disagreement - differences can be sorted out."

Change is very slow, but without that respect there would be no listening and no communication at all.

There is another important consideration concerning respect. Whenever we show respect we are acknowledging that what we respect is sacred. It is an important part of the whole of Creation, whether we understand its importance or not. We know there is a reason for its existence. We know, if we think deeply about it, that all life is sacred, that every human being is sacred. We can remind ourselves of that at any time by contemplating a little newborn baby. All over the world it is the same, regardless of color or culture, every little baby is a miracle that touches and opens our hearts with joy.

"Oh!" we exclaim, "how sweet, how beautiful! The tiny fingers and toes, the big wondering eyes gazing at us – aw! How absolutely loveable!" We want to hold her, and when her little hand grasps our finger, we melt. We marvel at the innocence, the complete goodness of this tiny being. With reflection we must understand that everyone in the world was just like this once, that every human being must partake of that basic goodness. That many people may now exhibit bad qualities and do bad things should make us wonder what happened to them. If they were born good they did not just suddenly decide to do bad things. Something happened to them at very early ages, at times when they were unable to understand or deal with what was done to them, and they had no one to support and help them.

I have been counseling prisoners for a quarter of a century, and I know this to be true. No matter what terrible things they may have done it has not destroyed the basic human goodness with which they were born. But they came to believe they were bad because of how they were treated, which caused them to do bad things that reinforced that belief. None of them were respected as children. They were ignored or punished or abandoned or manipulated or abused or criticized or blamed or bought off, but never respected. Never ever treated as a sacred and important child of Creation.

But in our circle they were respected. Probably for the first time in their lives. They were not respected at home, at school, by teachers, counselors, social workers, police, lawyers, judges, and certainly not in jail. The agreement of the circle is to respect each other. That has a profound impact, creates a safe space of understanding and trust, where it is possible for each to glimpse and seek to recover the hurt but good little child that still hides inside each one.

It should be clear to everyone that our first instruction must be respect. Most people if you asked them would agree to that. But usually they think of it in terms of their not getting enough respect, not in terms of their giving it to others or to the non-human beings in Creation..

But what a change would come in the world if human beings really returned to their first instruction of respect! We would stop tearing up the earth, cutting the ancient growth of trees and the rain forests, stop polluting the air and water, stop driving whole species of living beings to extinction. We would sit down with our enemies and listen respectfully to each other to solve our differences with words instead of weapons, as the Houdonousonie, the People of the Longhouse, have done since they adopted the Great Law of Peace many hundreds of years ago.

It seems a good sign to me that the new president, Barack Obama, has said he respects his opponents, people with differing viewpoints, and will listen to them. That alone shold be a refreshing hange for America.

When the Vietnamese Buddhist monk Thich Nhat Hanh was asked after the terrorist attacks of September, 2001, what he would say to Osama Bin Laden, he said exactly what I would say: "I would listen to him."

If everyone followed the instruction of respect we would give good attention to each member of our community, to every child, every adult, every elder. Instead of spreading conflict, fear, grief, destruction and death, we would begin to create harmony, peace, love, joy, beauty and life. Those things all human beings desire.

Things to think about: Do you respect yourself? Do you treat your body like the precious gift that it is? Do you give it enough rest, put only healthy things in it, move

16

it enough? Are there other people who do not have your respect? Why not – do you think you know everything about them? Remember respect doesn't mean liking, only the agreement to listen with an open mind and learn about the person. Do you listen to your children, to your parents and other family members respectfully? Are you respecting all life on Earth in your daily practises regarding pollution and energy use?

It is true that love is ultimately what we all seek. It is the greatest experience of human life, and it is even more important for us to give it than it is to receive it. But before we can love others, we must love ourselves, be relaxed and enjoy ourselves, be our own best friend. And love can only be based in respect.

The elders I have sat with, travelled with, who opened their homes to me, also opened their hearts. They embodied respect in every breath, and it was from that unfailing respect that they enveloped me in kindness and in love. In living this instruction they not only showed themselves, they showed me myself.

Through respecting ourselves we can learn of our own goodness, learn to love ourselves as precious, sacred gifts of Creation, giving us the serenity to walk peacefully, confidently, joyfully, in a sacred manner on a good road. Through respecting others, knowing deeply their real goodness, we can have positive, supportive, warm and fulfilling relationships. It is about our relationship, our living together in a good way on the Earth. This we will understand from the next instruction – the Circle.

RESPECT

See that ant
Got work to do
Don't see what or why
But he's at it
I respect that

And that little mouse there
Chewing up my sweater
Making a nest
May as well let him
He's got a family
I respect that

I've had worse
Head lice crab lice
Pin worms
They say
We all carry parasites
I'm probably full of them
Living in me off me

Well okay I'm living
Off Mother Earth
Guess these little guys
Are all family too
I respect that

Let's just not kill the host
Eh? Or hostess....

2. THE CIRCLE: RELATIONSHIP

One of the most important understandings of the elders is that all existence is relationship. Nothing is separate in existence. No one is alone. When we say "all my relations", we are reminding ourselves that we are related to all that is in Creation. When we say "we are relatives" we mean you and me and the earth, the sun, the stars, everything in the great circle of the universe.

The form of the circle is central to this thinking. As old Nick Black Elk noted, the earth, moon, sun and stars are all circles and move in circles, the greatest power of wind and water, in cyclones and maelstroms, are in spirals. Black Elk said that when his people were strong and happy it was the result of living in a circle: the Sacred Hoop of the nation, he called it. When that circle was broken by the invasion of the Europeans, people began to be lost. The native nations and communities were torn apart, torn from sacred homelands, torn from ancient ways and ceremonies. People lost both home and livelihood, and worst of all, lost each other. Now the people have the highest rate of poverty, of unemployment, of alcoholism and suicide, of any ethnic group in America. The elders sadly note that, like the invaders, they have lost their instructions.

But the people who survived this North American holocaust, where over 80 million people perished in four centuries, have begun to mend the sacred hoop again, to come together, to revive ancient ceremonies, songs and stories, to help each other, to find the spirit path, the Good Red Road.

We gather in circles for our ceremonies. This reminds us that we are all equal on this earth. The circle has no top or bottom. No greater or lesser. It has no beginning and no end, so exists in infinity and eternity. We orient our circles to four directions and note our progress through them in our lives: dawn, midday, sunset, midnight; birth, youth, adulthood, old age; spring, summer, fall, winter.

In the woodlands of our people we have a sacred circle. The former chief of our Assonet band Windsong Alden Blake and I searched these woods when we were both much younger and found a place where the trees had left a circlular space just the right size to hold our ceremonies. We built a sacred fire there, and our people built an arbor around it where the elders and our families could sit, which we refurbish every year. We also have a community house on the reservation to hold circles in inclement weather.

In our circles at home the women enter through the eastern door and sit in the south, the men come through the western door and sit in the north. There is a balance across the fire in the center. First the men speak, giving the women the last word. The elders of each sex speak first, as they have a long perspective and perhaps much to offer. In this way we honor their lives, service, and wisdom. But we value equally the thoughts of the young who may have new ideas, as well as the observations of the adults who are doing most of the work of the community.

We also may have other smaller circles to bring parts of the community closer and focus on different perspectives. There may be clans who might be responsible for certain ceremonies or other considerations. There may be councils of elders, women councils, men councils, considering many aspects of community life and responsibilities.

It was not only Black Elk's people, the Oglala Lakota, who were strong and happy living in a circle. It appears to be that the earliest creatures we call human lived in circles. The remains of ancient ancestors buried millions or year ago have been found interred respectfully: elders buried with honor together with their prized possessions. This indicates a community cooperating with each other, having sacred rites, and some sense of a destination beyond the grave. The most ancient artifacts, carvings and cave paintings show much involvement with animals. Weapons appear to be for hunting, as there are not any indications of inter-tribal warfare or conflict. No scenes of the domination of human beings by others of their kind. All the way to the beginnings of civilization and urban centers there are images of animals and plants, fruit and grain, and of female spirits, goddesses perhaps, fertility figures being praised and honored.

All over the world people moved in small groups, spreading from Africa up into Asia Minor, north and west into Europe, east into India, the Far East, and to Australia and the Pacific Islands. Wherever they stopped they built their small communities, always cooperating, as the survival of the individual depended on the survival of the group. That was the instruction they all understood. Human culture grew globally in this way: The community, the tribe, the village, was the center, the heart and the spirit of human life. It was a circle. That is, each was an equal part of the whole. And they understood that this whole included the earth and the larger unknown circle of spirit beyond.

This way of life conformed to what our elders called the Original Instructions for human beings. Living in a circle they cared for one another, together, as one being with one spirit. They cared for all their beloved children as the children of all. Together they cared for the old ones who could no longer care for themselves, the grandmothers and grandfathers of the community. Together they cared for the injured and the sick. Women worked together for the community, and men worked together. Groups grew within the tribe, each with a primary allegiance to the whole community. Each relationship was guided by a spirit that was part of the spirit of the tribe: between adults and children, between friends and lovers, within families and clans. It was "one for all and all for one".

Living in such a culture, being born and raised in it, gives the individual a totally different understanding (of himself, of relationship, of society and of life) from that of all people today who have been raised in a culture of individualism and competition, of struggle and conflict and isolation, of insecurity and the threat of violence, of a desperation for love and touch, of self-inflicted wants and needs for material things to fill their emptiness.

The scope of that lack of understanding is clear to me when I read the pronouncements and theories of anthropology and sociology discussing the life of tribal peoples today or of pre-history. The attitudes revealed are those of a culture in which man is considered as an individual, albeit conditioned by his society. Tribal peoples are spoken of as though they were isolated individuals or members of nuclear families. These did not exist. It is clear to me that nearly all the concepts of pre-historical life are skewed by this unaware bias. They are wrong.

The tribal peoples, living so intimately with the earth and the other creatures, held them to be of great importance, to be sacred, and they saw the spirit of the tribe in that intimate connection. Therefore they understood they were not only relatives in a tribe that must care for each other, but also relatives of the earth and all its inhabitants, with a responsibility also to care for them.

The governing condition of living as a member of a circle has consequences that are crucial to the relations and social interactions of the tribe. When you are born and raised in a circle contained by other circles, in an extended family, in a clan, a compound, a village, you come to know well the human beings there as they affect your life and growth. There are no strangers, no institutions or bureaucratic entities interrupting or intersecting life in the circle. Among most tribal peoples visitors have always been treated with courteous respect and with a joyous hospitality. Besides having natural curiosity about strangers, tribal people tend to be open and friendly and eager to create bonds of friendship.

That, of course, was the downfall of most of the tribes being invaded by dissembling foreigners pretending to come in friendship in order to get an advantage for conquest. Something the tribal people knew nothing about and could not imagine, since they were content to live in peace in their own lands.

But being born and growing in a secure circle of people who know and trust and depend on each other has this significant effect: it encourages what is most human in us.

What is that? What are the qualities that are truly human? This is an essential question for people today who have lost their Original Instructions. Since all adults have been heavily conditioned by their culture, we can only see what we may call our natural humanness in very young children before the ways of the world have begun to twist and distort their responses to life. We must observe little babies and tiny infants as they arrive newborn and fresh from Creation.

21

One of the first things we notice is a strong curiosity which is coupled with a wonderful ability to learn quickly. Other animals show some curiosity and some ability to learn from the environment, but they are much more limited to only what is at hand and useful for the needs of the moment.. Much of their guidance is instinctual, from Original Instructions imbedded in their genes. But human intelligence from the first moments of life seems to want to learn and discover and understand more and more, and to inquire of the meaning and significance of things.

Another thing we can notice about newborns is that they are very pleased to be here, very excited to be alive. You can observe this sparkling in their eyes. They do more than simply learn about their environment, they actively enjoy it. Human beings are not born sad or depressed, they arrive with a fully developed capacity for joy. They are active and eager to be involved and to have fun. They want to play, and they turn their world into a playground, everything into a toy. They laugh a lot. Especially when you play with them.

In a while we notice the interaction of the baby with others. Initially they are entirely open to meet others, having no expectations, only curiosity. Unless and until they feel something threatening from others they are completely trusting. When we smile at them they smile happily back, and they laugh when we play with them and want to engage us more in that way. They are spontaneous and immediate about expressing other feelings to us as well. They want to communicate and to be understood. They let us know when they are hungry or uncomfortable or tired. They hold nothing back when they feel safe and want to be close to others, to be seen and understood, and to be lovingly touched.

Eventually feelings of caring and concern for others come also spontaneously without being taught. Children who feel safe and loved are naturally tender, gentle, and loving towards parents, siblings, other members of the family and community, and to small animals.

One other human trait seems to arrive naturally to all children as they grow and learn. That is to create. They begin to sing, to dance, to tell stories, to make useful or beautiful things.

What of the negative qualities that have been called human? Such as greed, envy, laziness, gluttony, dissembling, violence, destructiveness, hatred, and so on. The deadly sins, however many, that still plague our world.

We do not find these in newborns. They begin to develop after the child has encountered adult reactions and criticism of the baby's innocent wants and enthusiasm. Children may then experience hurts from which they have no loving assistance to recover. Children with a resource of caring people to help them through the inevitable traumas do not carry these negative emotions further into life.

22

The Original Instructions of living in a circle provide that there will always be a caring person at hand for the child who will listen with compassion and assure the child she only needs to express what she feels and the hurt will pass, that she is good, and strong, and smart, and capable and completely loveable, and that despite the pain of that moment life will go on being good and manageable. When the children spontaneously express their feelings, are heard and understood and encouraged, they are quickly forgotten, and the children move on. They don't want to hold on to uncomfortable feelings, they want to have fun, to laugh and to play.

Children who don't have this resource, who have no one to run to, will not finish with the hurt. Without a friendly guide they do not understand what to do with these feelings, how to safely express the hurts to someone who can assure them they are completely good and loveable, that they are not alone, have support and assurance they can handle whatever they need to. Without such resource and support, when they feel alone and abandoned, they retreat and store the confusing feelings. They will forget them, but they stay in unconscious memory and will return, making them once more alone and confused. Children who are neglected or abused will pile up these old hurts inside them, and they will turn toxic and poison from within with negative emotions and destructive patterns of behavior.

A child born to a community that welcomes her as one of its own, a community of peaceable, caring people who respect and attend each other in willing cooperation, who listen to every child and who guide them with loving care (a community, in other words, of real human beings) such a child will feel very safe to be herself and to express herself spontaneously and easily to anyone in that circle. Her natural human qualities are curiosity and intelligence, fun and joy in living, spontaneous expression, and affection and creativity, and these are all encouraged by the caring, the safety and the trust of the people of her circle.

A child born to such a community will be able to express and so leave behind the hurts and negative feelings that arise. Because the community is small enough that the people are all known to each other and care for and about each other, because they function best by cooperation and open communication and listen to each one, respect and encourage each one, their human qualities are enhanced and negative ones minimized.

This is not the picture described in the imaginations of anthropology scholars who see and understand human nature in the way people do who were raised in the brutal, violent, competitive world of lonely individuals navigating dangerous waters of greed, envy, sloth, and so on. The novels and the films using those texts present us with images of savagery, jealousy, domination and warfare among tribes. This is dramatic and commercial, but there is scant evidence for such a picture except the extrapolation the authors make from what they see as "human nature" today.

I don't believe in that kind of "human nature" at all. What I have experienced of what is left of tribal living today indicates a very different view of the lives of our ancient ancestors. I see people who are kindly, tolerant, friendly, hospitable, humorous, relaxed and easy-going, enjoying family, friends, nature, and simple pleasures.

So I really don't believe in all that drama and violence and conflict.

When people talk about struggles in the tribes and warfare among them, they are only making assumptions based on what we see of human interactions today. I believe that they lived in circles, in balance with each other, in harmony with nature. Certainly it is true that before the Europeans came and set upon our nations in North America, most of them lived peacefully with themselves and their neighbors.

(Of course, what I am saying is a generalization. Tribes have personalities just as individuals do, and sometimes we may run across tribes that have strayed far from original human nature, isolated bands that have become neurotic or even sociopathic. You ask the reason for that? Well, the human mind, varied and complex as it is, can be a delicate thing. As a series of relentless hurts and pressures can turn a man against his fellows when he has no caring support, he may, in violence and aggression, if he is powerful enough, upset the balance of supports in the community. Using his power and terror to manipulate others, he may be able to create and systematize dissention and undermine support, destroy closeness that permanently damages the equality, cooperativeness and caring of that tribe. Aggression, violence, the need for power can unbalance and actually make a tribe crazy.)

My opinions here are shaped by my travels among the many first nations of Turtle Island, talking with elders, hearing their stories, the histories of their peoples. From that evidence and the evidence of my own experience of the people I have the conviction that what I tell you now is truth, which is far different from the unsupported suppositions of the texts we were taught in the conqueror's schools.

When I see our communities that survive, the ones maybe a bit removed from the swathe of conquest, who have been able to retain some of the old ways, I can feel that line going back to our ancestors, following the Original Instructions. I see a people, a good people, naturally caring for the land, connected to plant life, to animals, birds, fish, to the winds the rain, the thunderers, to the seasons in their circle. I see a people at home with themselves and each other, relaxed and full of humor, watching the children grow, attending the old ones who dream their lives again.

I see a million years and more. The earth rolling around the sun. The people sitting around a fire, telling stories, wondering about the stars. They are not fighting each other. They have always been together and they care for each one there in that circle and know they belong there. The beloved elders have brought them to here, and now they care for them and show their gratitude. The little ones asleep are the delight of their days and the hope of the years that will come.

And the land they walk, the land they sleep upon, it is their home, their mother, a generous provider when they honor and follow her guidance. And all the other creatures are following their instructions so they may all live upon this land in a good way.

When they meet other bands as they move about on this land there is absolutely no reason to be anything but friendly. This is the human being way. Their languages may be different, but they can communicate well in signs and with vocal tones and facial expressions. There is nothing to fight about. They recognize each other as peaceable bands living together in cooperation, sharing, and caring for each other. They bear no wealth - it is in the land and there for all.

People conditioned by our culture think it would be human for those people to quarrel and to fight each other. I say, and this is from direct observation of the circle way of life, it would be human for them to be hospitable to strangers, to be friendly and curious, and to learn from each other. This is exactly what was reported by the Europeans in almost all of their first encounters with the native peoples of North America. That is how it was for all people before the coming of civilization. The problems of domination and conflict and violence didn't appear for the first few million years of humanoid existence on the planet. Not until seven to ten thousand years ago. But that's another story for another time.

The important thing passed down to us from the old ones is that the Original Instructions are for human beings to live in a circle. The circle provides elements that people require in order to stay human. That is why our elders considered it one of the essential Original Instructions for human beings. The systems we live under and must contend with are not circles and they inhibit and reduce our humanity. Have you ever tried to get a human response out of a subordinate of a large institution? A compassionate, caring response – or even reason? They cannot give human responses and must remain subordinate out of fear of losing their positions.

Because fear is the energy that holds together a domination system, as opposed to a cooperation system. Human beings became human, became *homo sapiens sapiens* by cooperating. Cooperation was the relationship devised by our weak and vulnerable hominid ancestors to protect and provide for themselves. For an individual to join a cooperation group it had to agree to work for the benefit of each one. Men, women, old, young, physically strong or weak, mentally fast or slow, the group had to protect and provide for all. It is natural for people living close to each other, growing up together cooperating for the same ends, to

25

be affectionate and playful and enjoy each other. Absolutely natural as long as everyone treats everyone well and all needs are respected.

We live in an inhuman society, a society of institutions, from government to business to education and health, which are pyramids. Power comes from the top, from the elite few who control the wealth and resources of the Earth. It is a society which, rather than supporting people, pits people against each other. Rather than a system of cooperation and equality, it is a system of competition, domination and subordination. Rather than bringing people together it separates and divides. Rather than valuing love and compassion, creativity and learning and the beauty of the natural world, it turns people into consumers who are taught that happiness lies in wealth and status.

What is the result of this alienation? Drugs, crime, violence, terrorism, war. Children shooting children in schools. People opening fire on strangers in restaurants, strapping explosives to themselves to detonate in the market. Street gangs. Road rage. Abduction and rape of children. Sex industries. Dictators. Military juntas. Governments that lie, torture and ignore human rights. Justice systems that can be bought. Corruption in both business and government, in Wall Street. Oppression of the poor, the weak, of children, women, minorities. Genocide. Wiping out whole species and destroying the Earth.

This is what we think is normal. We say it's just human nature.

It's not. It's insanity. It's dehumanization. It's a civilization warped and twisted away from the trend of millions of years of evolution with more complex, rational, creative thought and into the madness of blind, unthinking rage, terror, and desperation. That's what happens when our human family is destroyed, when there is no closeness and understanding, no mutual support and kindness, and people are left to wander friendless and alone in a hostile world.

The circle has the power to heal all that. It is a way that has worked for us in the past, and works well even today, in the worst of our places, in the prisons, when we bring that circle to our people there, it begins to heal them. To see how it touches the prisoners who have been so deeply damaged by this domination system and its inhumanity, and how they begin to recover their own humanity, the hopeful, caring, thoughtful, playful little children they once were, is always astounding, but every week of my life I witness such healing in our circles. And I see nothing else working so deeply, quickly and thoroughly.

The African philosophy of ubuntu teaches that all people are dependent on each other. According to ubuntu, a person only becomes a person through other people.

"The solitary, isolated human being is a contradiction in terms," writes Nobel Peace Prize winner Bishop Desmond Tutu, "Because we need one another, our natural tendency is to be cooperative and helpful. If this were not true we would have died out as a species a long time ago, consumed by our violence and hate."

Things to think about: can you make a circle with your family or others you may live with? Is there a friend you could introduce to the idea of a circle – of agreeing to respect each other and listen supportively to each other? Could you suggest with friends and co-workers a special time when you all speak with trust and honesty about your deepest concerns, everyone listening supportively and no one speaking twice until everyone has spoken once? Can you imagine such a circle meeting regularly and taking up projects to support one another, to enhance family and community life, working and playing together?

Whenever I was together with elders we were a circle. Sometimes it was formally begun, sometime it just naturally fell together that way. Since then it has always felt natural to me to form a circle with whomever I am with, even if there are only two of us – we take turns speaking and listening, never interrupting, never speaking twice until everyone else has been heard. In that way assertive people are encouraged to listen and think more, and non-assertive people are allowed greater freedom to express themselves.

Two of the things people most often mention as missing in today's culture that they long for are family and community. People have a sense that at some time in the past the families were strong and close and supportive, and they were together in communities that were the same. And so it was.

In my international family summer camps the European people experience living for a week or two in the old way, tribally, in circles, and it changes them. We use circles of varying sizes to bring people together and build trust, openness and intimacy. At the end of camp people often say they can't believe that they got so close so quickly to complete strangers, closer, in fact, than they have been to their own friends and family, because they have taken the time in small circles to really listen to each other. They begin to heal from the stresses of the isolating, competitive society. They start to find themselves and the gifts of Creation they are meant to give away.

Often they continue to meet during the year with their small circles, some have found ways to live together, others are impatient until next year to feel the healing of a circle. They begin to dream of how to make such a community in which to live the rest of their lives. They have begun to know this is their way, the human-being way to live. To think and dream and plan how to make their lives together in the Circle Way, following the Original Instructions.

A SONG FOR OUR CIRCLE

Today we circle together again
To make another work,
So I want my song today
To celebrate our circle.

Our ingredients: babies crying,
Being held and fondled,
Their fear and rage respected,
We're only pleased and fond;

Children running, laughing, raucous,
Falling, scrambling, hiding,
Exploding, energy photons darting
Orbiting the heart of the tribe.

People sitting on their blankets,
Feeling the grass beneath,
Elders leaning back in chairs,
Wrapped in shawls and memories.

Below a few lazy clouds, birdsong
Tossing about the breeze,
Insects hum the chorus, warming
Sunlight through shady trees,

And if the weather be cold or wet,
We feed a common fire,
Kindling a glow on every face,
Flaring our souls' desires.

Just when the joy of being close
Seems too much to take,
We safely can retire a while
Behind some tea and cakes.

Other's stories touch our own,
Their tears salt our eyes.
We live and taste and ponder again
The strangeness of our lives.

Giving attention to every moment,
To every blade of grass,
Grains of sand, drops of ocean,
That wistful look in the glass.

Long ago the conquerors came,
Tore us from our Mother,
All our lives we searched for home;
At last we found each other.

Against confusion we always knew
No matter what the weather,
How we need each other so
From then we are together.

Our circle is a place where each
Of us has our song,
Here we know we are needed,
And here we all belong.

3. THANKSGIVING

Among our people the term we translate as "prayer" means something different than it seems to mean in many religions and cultures. For us, our prayers are always giving thanks, not asking for things. Even when we are praying for someone who is sick or injured or in difficulty we are not so much asking for some power to intercede as we are just giving voice to our compassion. Rather than use this word prayer, more often our people will call the act by its truer name, thanksgiving. "Let us join in a thanksgiving," we will say, or "Grandfather, will you give the thanksgiving for us?"

In the way that I was taught there are two parts to this expression, greetings and thanksgivings. The greetings we discussed above, reminding ourselves of our relationships, connecting with our relatives. Then the thanks for the many gifts we receive. Whatever we require for our survival Mother Earth supplies us, all our food, shelter, fuel, clothing, medicine, whatever we need, so first we thank her. Then we thank the plant and animal as well as all our human relatives for all their many gifts and for what they teach us. We also thank the beings beyond the earth in the great circle of the universe. We are happy they are all doing what they were put there to do, following their instructions, and all is in order and well at this time. And finally we must acknowledge that Power that is responsible for it all, that great Unknown, Source of everything, including life itself. Even though it is a mystery forever beyond our comprehension, we are truly grateful. We are so happy this Creation exists, and that we have been given the great honor and privilege to be alive and aware of this experience for even just a few of the billions of turnings of our earth around the sun. And so we, with all our hearts and minds, offer at last our greetings and our thanksgivings to the Creator. We feel so blessed we want to give thanks, give thanks, give thanks, for every moment of life is a treasure, a sacred gift.

The elders realize how prone we sometimes become to take this gift for granted. "For granted," a strange expression. Granted means given. That means once we have given thanks for a gift it is enough. Except that life is the gift that keeps on giving, and if we for any moment forget that it is a gift and that without it there would be nothing, then we have lost the true joy of that moment forever

How much it would add to us, to our understanding as well as to our happiness, if we could remember just to stop at times and give thanks. When we wake up and greet the day, and when we have concluded some piece of our work. Certainly before we sit to eat. But also when we feel tired or stressed or worried or upset or confused or overwhelmed – giving thanks at those times provides us with a totally new perspective.

If only we could make it a regular practice to stop then and take a deep breath. Then take another and think of the gift it is to have a body that feeds on that air, that we have that oxygen that renews our blood, that our hearts are beating and sustaining us. That the earth is still living and caring for us, the grass still green, the trees still sprouting leaves and then gifting them to the soil. That there is beauty all around us. That we have the stories of yesterday, the challenges of today, and the dreams of tomorrow.

Then we can take another deep breath of this life and say to it, "It's a great time to be alive! Thank you, Creator."

The warriors on the plains of old would say, "It's a good day to die." That too. When we are living well it is always a good day to die. Good to recognize our life has had a purpose, and that by following our instructions we have fulfilled that purpose and can die happy, having done our best. But it is also a good day to live, to keep doing our best and follow our instructions on a good red road. It is good to stop often and give thanks, because when we do we remind ourselves of those instructions and that it is by following them that we always see and feel the beauty of each moment.

The elders urged us to give thanks, and they were a model for us in that. They began every time they spoke by giving thanks. They thanked Creator and all our relatives. They thanked us for being there, and when they finished they thanked us for listening. And so we tried to follow their example, and it did make a difference in our lives.

I think, when they were young, our elders were like us, full of bravado, hiding feelings of anxiety, confusion, ignorance, inadequacy. But they listened to their elders, and they learned it was right and important to give thanks and to give thanks often. And so we began to follow that instruction, because it seemed to be a central part of their understanding. The more we succeeded in giving thanks, the more often we did that, the more it changed us, the more it gave us support and strength, and the more it connected us to the spirit of Creation.

Now that I have become an elder myself, I have learned to stop and appreciate Creation and all its beauty and give thanks very often through my waking hours. The effect even enters my sleep and makes my dreaming clear and strong. Like most old people I experience the speeding up of life. The last seven decades seem to have raced past, faster and faster, and now that my eighth decade is drawing to a close, I want more than ever to slow down the passage of time and hold each precious moment lovingly and thoughtfully. I am happy to have so many vivid memories of my early years, which I guess is why us old folks spend so much time remembering the old times. But then I began to keep a journal to encourage myself to stop and recall the days as they fly by. And I also see that the more often I stop in my day and breathe deep of life and give thanks, the more I slow down and relish and cherish these precious hours of living.

There are other things for which I have discovered it important to give thanks. It's easy, really, to give thanks to this wonderful earth that is our home and keeps sustaining us. It's easy to give thanks for the grass and the trees, for the water and the air, for our animal relatives, and even for all struggling humanity, as we are part of all that. What is more difficult is to give thanks to particular individuals. As someone once said, "I love humanity, it's only people I can't stand,"

It is people, other human beings, who hurt us the most. If a bee stings us our feelings are not hurt, and we are not angry at the whole species. But when a person hurts us we are apt to carry that hurt in our hearts. If enough people hurt us, we may decide to trust no one and to keep to ourselves.

What I have learned by making circles in the prisons for twenty years is that when people hurt you it is because they were hurt themselves. I said this earlier, but I feel I need to say it often. It is such an important fact that we rarely if ever consider. Yet we must consider it, for when we are born we are all innocent and good, and no baby or small child wants to hurt anyone. Not until he has been hurt himself. Then he learns, out of his upset feelings, to hurt back. If he carries those upset feelings in his heart he may begin to hurt people who never hurt him, or anyone. Even then, I have learned, he does not really want to hurt or mistreat others, but he is driven to it by feelings he does not understand and doesn't know how to control.

Under all the hurt, the bad and nasty feelings that a person may carry with him, there still exists that innocent little baby that only wanted to live and be loved. I know this, because I have seen the most hardened criminals, real tough guys, discover again that goodness and innocence and caring buried at the bottom of their own hearts.

I'll write another book about that some time, if Creation gives me time for it, but this is important for us all to understand. These criminals would not have gone on their hard black road if, when they were small babies and children, someone had been there for them, someone who truly cared about them, who respected their thoughts and feelings, who listened to them when they were hurt and who told them they were good and valuable human beings and helped them to follow the good red road. We must remind ourselves and each other continually always to be aware of the natural goodness of every human being.

Children in this dominant society hear a lot about what's wrong with them and very little about what is wonderful about them. How shall they grow to be wonderful adults if no one reflects that to them? We learn and grow the fastest by positive reinforcement. And after we are grown to adulthood not many people tell us how good we are, how well we are doing, how much they like and admire us. But many people are very ready to point out where we fail, ready to criticize and find fault and judge us. Many are prone to speak badly about us to others, to "badmouth" us.

Our society has too much of "badmouthing". In close-knit groups like our Native communities it can eat like a cancer at the people's trust and love. I want to propose a new expression: "Goodmouthing."

Goodmouthing is a concept grounded in our old Original Instruction of thanksgiving. When we stop to give thanks we are remembering the things that we appreciate. We think of the reasons why we love the sun and moon and the stars, our beautiful earth and all her children, and it makes us happy to remember the joys we find in all of them. When we praise our animal friends they like it and want to please us. When we praise the plants in our garden they grow stronger. When we appreciate our loved ones, our friends, or even strangers, it makes them feel very good, and that makes us happy too.

So in my camps and workshops I have created a special form for this which I call an appreciation circle. It works like this:

The first one to take the talking stick (or feather or shell or whatever) must tell the circle something he likes about himself, and then each of the others in the circle gets to tell him something they like about him. The first part is the hardest for most of us, because we have been rightly taught not to be boastful and to show humility. That is certainly good teaching, fitting our Original Instructions, as you may consider in my chapter, "Humility". But I tell everyone this is not about boasting. People boast and brag when they are insecure. When they doubt themselves and demand reassurance. When they feel, deep inside, there is something not right about them, so they have to keep calling attention to themselves. They are out of balance, and so they want to assert, not that they are equal, but that they are better than others.

Of course we don't like to hear that. But it would be good to remind ourselves that when someone tries to seem better than others, the poor fellow really thinks he is not as good. By boasting he is his own worst enemy, because no one likes that.

So we must understand this is not about boasting. Not about being better than anyone. It is about giving thanks to the Spirit of Creation that gave us life. It is about appreciating the gifts we have been given. It is not boasting to speak of a talent you have been blessed with. If you have developed that, you are honoring the Creator's gift. If you are kind and caring and a good child to your parents, a good friend, a good parent to your children, these are traits you were born with. It is good to acknowledge them. They are reality, and you can be both grateful and humble about that.

It is said that it is easier to love others when we love ourselves. Well, if you love yourself it shouldn't be so hard to say something good about yourself. When we get bitten by that love bug we want to stop strangers on the street to tell them how wonderful our beloved is. And when you have a hard time learning how to love yourself, if you force yourself to think about your best points, your strengths , and make yourself tell someone what you like about yourself, you will be reinforcing those good thoughts and feelings and learning to like yourself more.

I tell everyone to contradict their natural shyness and fears of seeming boastful, to be bold and positive and tell their good qualities in a relaxed, matter-of-fact way. And remember that Creator made you that way, gave you those gifts, and you are only acknowledging and appreciating those gifts. And I tell the circle to encourage each one to be very positive in appreciating herself, and that it is good to be proud of the gifts Creation has given each of us. It is a celebration – when we celebrate ourelves we are celebrating life celebrating the Creation.

Then the person continues to hold the stick and sit quietly and listen to the things other people in the circle appreciate about him. There's only one real rule I give for this appreciation circle and that is that when you are listening to someone giving you an appreciation you are not allowed to speak. You can laugh or cry or stare at the floor, but you cannot answer back. You must only take it in. Only when they have finished can you say, "thank you."

I ask the small clan groups to make appreciation circles at the end of our workshops and camps. They are usually the high point and certainly one of the most memorable evens of the seminars and camps. We have appreciation circles as a celebration for a person's birthday, or other life events like graduations, promotions, weddings, and funerals. Because there is so much "badmouthing", criticism, and judgement that we hear all the time it is truly wonderful to listen to people appreciate each other. It is a joy to think about the good qualities each person has and to let that person know you have noticed and appreciate them. And it often comes as a shock and a surprise to hear some of the good things that other people think about you.

Thanksgiving is a celebration. And, like all acts of celebration, we can learn to do it better and better, learn to make the act stronger and more effective. We don't do it much and are not very skilled at it yet. So it is good to look at, to study and improve our thanksgiving continually.

Here are some of the things I have discovered so far in this practise. It is good to be very positive. Not wishy-washy, or conditional when giving appreciations – to yourself or to others. It's good to be enthusiastic.

34

But it must be absolutely sincere. Not exaggerated. It may seem like an exaggeration because most of us are really better than we believe we are. (People who exaggerate their own importance are of course really insecure and don't believe in themselves – it's only a show – not their fault.)

It's good to notice change, to congratulate small succeses as people try to improve themselves. Our noticing that encourages it.

It's much better when we can be specific. What is it that the other person has (or you have, if you are appreciating yourself) done that you appreciate? What does it do for you? How does it make you feel? The other person will understand, accept, and appreciate your thanks much more when it is specific.

Try to avoid seeming to be giving a good grade, to be dangling a carrot, giving a gold star or a medal, that could seem like manipulation. A compliment to get something out of them. Judgements, whether positive or negative, only reinforce judgementalism. We don't want to be sitting in judgement on each other, only enjoying each other. Celebrating our pleasure in each other.

When I perceive that someone feels inadequate in some respect, I try to think of things that person does that contradict that notion. For instance, if someone seems afraid to be seen or heard by others and is acting out a pattern of shyness, I will direct her attention to times she has stepped a bit out of that shyness and spoken up. I will appreciate her bravery, because I know it is not easy for her.

Even if the person is a total stranger, there is something about him I might notice that gives me a good feeling, so I push myself to let him k now – he has a smile that makes me feel liked, or his eyes show he is interested in what I am saying, and so on.

It will help if you practise this. Make appreciation part of your conscious interaction with friends or strangers. You will get better at it, and it will show in the quality of interactions and relationships.

So. If it's a person you are appreciating, think about your appreciation before you give it. Not a judgement. Not an evaluation. Just exactly what did she do, what did that do for you, and how do you feel about it?

It's also important for us to know how to receive thanks and appreciation with grace. Isn't it strange how we dismiss thanks? We say, "Don't mention it." "No problem." "It was nothing" - Nada. Niente.

We have all gotten poor at being able to express our feelings. For some it is nearly impossible. We need to practise and this is an excellent way. To notice and actually express positive feelings to ourselves and others. It just makes life better. Gives pleasure, enjoyment, satisfaction, even relief. What a grand gift to be giving yourself and everyone!

Imagine a whole society where "badmouthing" of any kind was frowned upon, where "goodmouthing", appreciation and thoughtfulness were the normal ways in which people reacted to each other. A society in which people were only supportive of each other, encouraging each other, and showing their joy in each other. Where parents only appreciated and encouraged their children, were never critical or judgmental or manipulative or lecturing, but only showed their support, their belief and their faith in them. Where teachers and people in managerial positions were not focussed on the negative, on what their students and workers were doing wrong, but also on appreciating the good work, showing what was best and most successful, and trying to encourage the best in all of them. Where people anywhere were always willing to listen to you and validate you and empower you.

Things to think about: Whom do you appreciate in your life? How often do you express that appreciation to that person? How do you express it? Is there someone who may want to hear that appreciation? Is there someone you don't like very much? Can you think of things you could appreciate about that person? What might happen if you expressed that? Do you thank your family and friends, especially your children, just for being who they are? Do you give thanks when you wake up that you are given a new day of life? How about making a reminder to do that to set by your alarm clock?

Surveys of people who consider themselves happy find one trait they all have in common. Gratitude. Happy people are grateful, they focus on their thankfulness. They appreciate their lifes and all they have been given.. They feel blessed and they express that to themselves and others. They always see the glass as half-full – and optimists live longer. Fact.

A society using this way would be following the Original Instruction of Thanksgiving. Everyone would be recognizing the wonderful gifts of the Creator in herself and in everyone else. And by speaking of these to each other we would be making people happier, increasing the general atmosphere of happiness all around. In being of service to each other like this, we would also be in service to Creation.

Because when we direct our attention and the attention of others to the positive it inspires greater clarity of thought, insight, and creativity in all of us. It is a powerfully pro-evolution activity. It leads us always further towards a higher consciousness, one that is attuned to moving on the red road of the spirit, whose goal is the fulfillment of life's purpose and the purpose of Creation.

The elders I came close to not only gave thanks formally in every ceremony, they took pains to show appreciation to everyone they were with, everyone who helped them on their path, and they noticed and commented on the ways people helped others.

They were walking lessons in thanksgiving.

A THANKSGIVING PRAYER
(Watuppa Wampanoag Reservation, 1976)

O You who give all things
O Sacred Mystery
Behold us here, all your children
Gathered together this day once more
To rejoice and give you thanks

We thank you for the Sacred Gift
Of this life, the wonder-filled moment
And for our small tract in the Great Universe
For greening valleys, all holy mountains
For singing streams that feed vast waters
For the secrets of rain and snow and winds
That scatter the seeds and feed the furry roots
For the grass, the herbs, the flowers that heal
The trees that bend to feed and shelter us
Our little brothers and sisters of the animal nations
Thank you for our Grandfather Sun that warms
And fills all creatures with the power to grow
For Grandmother Moon that brings us dreams
For the cry of birth that fills the music of creation

Mystery, we thank you for our bodies with which
We see and hear, smell, taste and touch your world
We thank you for our minds by which
We adventure the many roads of learning
We thank you for our hearts' center by which
We know the joy, the sting, the sweet of love
And we thank you for the abiding spirits by which
We know beauty and the way of health

O You, who give all things
O Sacred Mystery
Behold us all your children
Gathered to celebrate and give thanks again
For living and knowing that we live
For learning more today the deepest secret
To walk your path for our brief time
In a sacred manner

A Final Word on Part One

I have placed these three instructions, Respect, the Circle, and Thanksgiving, at the beginning of this book partly because they are the ones that I have heard all my life the most often from the elders. But also because it seems to me they form the foundation of all teachings for human beings to live in a good way on this Earth. In practice I have seen that presenting only these three in our circles, in the prisons, at home on our reservation, traveling abroad, in schools, with young people everywhere, makes it clear and possible the way to happiness and to create a truly human society.

As a starting point for those teachings I have come to emphasize certain aspects of these three instructions. First, it seems important to begin with respecting ourselves. As I mentioned above, we know we cannot be fully loving until we love ourselves. We need to understand that we are engaged here in a magnificent story. We are all important actors in this drama, the children of glory, the crown of Creation. Every one of us is vital to the whole, and is therefore sacred. Seen in that light we must tender ourselves absolute respect. It is unfortunate that the domination culture we are all caught in has taught us falsely that there is something inherently wrong with human beings, that there is evil in our nature that we must expose and punish, that we are not good enough, sinful, guilty, worthy of blame. Now we have much work to do, to banish those destructive concepts from our thinking and our conditioning. We must make it a priority to achieve total self-respect in our worth as human beings.

Secondly, we need to realize we are not supposed to do all this alone, we need other human beings. We need closeness with other human hearts and the understanding of other human minds. Since this domination culture is set up to separate and isolate us from each other, we have work to do to bring us together again. Life is terrible when we have to fight each other, when we fear and cannot trust each other. And life is wonderful when we are with others who love and support us. Therefore we must begin to rebuild our circles as the center of our social system. Even in this alienating culture many of us have managed to make some pretty good relationships quite often. But I know that every one of us would like those relationships to be closer, more open, more supportive than they are, and we would like to have more of them. We have work to do there.

And thirdly, Thanksgiving, being truly thankful, will require some fundamental changes in our thinking, in our reactions and attitudes, which will in turn make all our relationships, including that to ourselves, easier and more rewarding. It requires us to end our ancient bad habits of criticism and complaint, of guilt and blame, of rewarding and punishing, of assigning good and bad, right and wrong to everything. It would help also to give up disappointment, which only saps our energy, and be thankful also for failures, as they add to our knowledge and make us smarter. When we can engage in absolute thanksgiving for every moment of life, welcome every failure and obstacle as a challenge and a learning, express complete appreciation of ourselves and of everyone else, how well we are doing in the face of great opposition, when we can be supportive of all people in their struggles, have empathy for their feelings and show them a true mirror of their worth, will that not be a wonderful world?

I have worked on these just enough and seen just enough progress in our work around us to have a glimpse of just how possible and how wonderful that world we are striving to build with each other will be. As it is, through eight decades of living I have been expanding in knowing and caring for myself, falling in love with everyone I meet and making more and closer connections, while treasuring every breath and every sacred moment of my life. The matured fruit of these teachings of my elders (and of my life) has developed into the process we call the Circle Way. The hearts that come to us yearning for life, for something to do, quickly learn this way and begin to transform and radiate love and joy and hope in new lives upon the path of the heart.

From my experience so far in teaching these three instructions I believe they are enough to change the world by themselves, but the other instructions that we will look at now can make that transition easier, richer, deeper, and help to undo the tragic setback of domination and put human beings back on the path of conscious evolution.

PART TWO

DIRECTION EAST – The Light of the Mind

ELEMENT AIR

Three instructions for evolution: qualities for becoming better at being human or

TO FIND AND FOLLOW A GOOD PATH IN LIFE

4. AWARENESS

5. HUMOR: PLAYFULNESS

· 6. HONESTY

PART TWO – THE EAST

Now it is the vernal equinox, on our Earth's annual circle dance around the sun – the time when day and night are equal and mark the advent of spring. Originally I thought to bring us to our people's most eastern area, the outer arm of Cape Cod, with its long and often wild Atlantic beach and giant dunes. It was a place familiar and important to my youth, and I feel at home there. But after I transcended the notion of staying in our tribal area, another eastern beach occurred to me, one I have only visited once but return to often in my mind and heart.

It is an island, long and narrow, called Assoteague, stretching from the eastern shores of Maryland down to Virginia. Like the Cape Cod Seashore it is protected and left natural, a nature preserve. I dreamed of coming here when I was a boy, and only a few years ago, already an old man, I was able to bring my wife here to share that dream.

We have come across from Chincoteague, parked at the Audubon headquarters where we could see exhibits and learn about the over 300 species of birds that find refuge here. But it is still dark, early in the morning. We have walked onto the great beach that stretches northward out of sight. We have timed it so that we can begin our circle on the beach at sunrise.

The stars sinking behind us are fading now as beyond the sea the sky grows light. Thin strips of cloud, tinged with pink, are turning gold. Let's just hold hands and come together a moment to feel the spirit of this place.

There is an endless song here, made of wind, cries of sea birds, and the incessant crumbling rollers of the Atlantic roughly caressing the level sands. Sometimes the song is tumultuous, explosive, during and after a great storm at sea, and sometimes it is a hush and a whisper, a lullaby from our ancient mother that may resonate in our minds. But always the song continues, and often when we have gone away, far inland, we still hear it through our dreams.

I wanted to be here with you because of the nature, because of the balance – man does not encroach here. No machines, noise, pollution – only one short road to the museum, the few visitors are not tourists, only nature lovers, bird watchers, and those like me – horse lovers. You will not see it on my face, but inside I will weep with happiness to see them again here, the wild horses of Assoteague. There are two herds, actually, one in the north of the island , one in the south. They do not overrun into each other's territories. It is believed they were once captives of human domination, brought here on a Spanish ship that wrecked off this coast, and their ancestors swam here, hundreds of years ago.

There they are! Completely free and independent of us. We watch from a distance, not allowed to enter their domain. They can ignore us. They are leaderless, but stay together, care for each other, have no conflicts – they are as human beings only long to be: free, equal and intimate – a family, a tribe. My heart opens and goes to them. We are cousins. I watch them from a distance, browsing and moving together as a tribe, and a surge of joy catches a lump in my throat and unbidden tears fill my eyes – they are so independent, so connected to each other and their land - so free! Protected on this island apart from our greedy civilization, they can peacefully live their Original Instructions.

The east, in my own usage of a medicine wheel, is a good place to pay attention to our thoughts. Here we greet our grandfather, as we call him, or elder brother as our Houdenasonie neighbors call him, the Sun. The Earth turns in sleep to have him look over her shoulder and wake her family. Bringing to us Wampanand, spirit of the East, of the Light, of the Dawn, of Birth and Renewal. The night was given to dreams, to fantasy, which may be hopeful or fearful. With the return of the light we can find reality again. We are alive. The world's still there. All is well.

We need the light to keep our thoughts grounded in truth, to banish the shadows that hide and distort reality. The human mind is a beautiful but delicate and vulnerable instrument. It is capable of great learning and creativity. But its clarity and balance require a grounding in reality. It is easily confused by misinformation, by lies and distortions of the truth. Abandonment or mistreatment in childhood, or even just the lack of friendly guidance, can install darkness and confusion in our minds that distort all future thought and action.

The three instructions that I have assigned to this direction therefore are Awareness, Humor, and Honesty, instructions our minds can adopt for becoming better at being human beings.

4. AWARENESS

There is an ancient saying that has been passed on to us by our elders, and I think of it often. To walk in a sacred manner, the saying goes, make every step upon the Earth Mother a prayer.

What does this mean, really? Of course, it suggests it would be best if we could be aware of the sacredness of existence in every moment. That is why whenever we come together we will greet our Mother Earth and feel her presence beneath us. She is a generous mother. And also very beautiful, and it makes us happy to look at her.

And then we greet her other children. It is so good we are not alone here on earth but have so many relatives living with us. There are all the plant people putting their roots into the Mother. They share so many gifts with us of food and medicine and materials we can use. Sometimes we greet certain favorites especially. In the spring the strawberry that brings us the first fruit, and in the summer the green corn. Then there are trees that are very sacred to us, the cedar and the white birch, and in late winter the sugar maple that gives us its sweet juice.

Then there are the animal relatives. Those that dig and burrow inside the earth, those that crawl and creep and run across her, those that swim in her waters, and those that fly through the air and climb the winds. We may mention some of those who are especially important to our lives. They bring many gifts and many lessons. Also there are those other two-leggeds, the human beings, struggling with their lives as we are, all over the earth.

Next we look out, beyond the earth, to the great circle of the sky. There we see the moon, whom we call grandmother, and we recall that she pulls the oceans back and forth and brings cycles of cleansing and fertility to our females. We mark times of ceremony by her changes and plant and harvest by them. She fills our thoughts with wonder and mystery and brings forth imagination and creativity. And we greet the sun, whom we often call grandfather, and remember without that relative no life could flourish, all would be dark and frozen.

Beyond, there are the star nations that appear when the sun has gone down. They keep their relationships the same, and by that we can recognize them as old friends who show us our directions on the earth as well as the passing of the hours through the night until dawn. And we are told these are only a few of our nearest neighbors, that they and we are part of a vast circle of stars indicated by that bright star path through the sky. And we are told this circle of billions of stars is only one of billions of such circles in the circle of the whole universe that is so big it is beyond the capacity of our little minds to comprehend.

But the instructions that guide them all however far they may be are the same as the instructions that we follow. And so we are part also of that one great circle and we are all relatives.

Most important after all that, is for us to recognize that there is something more. All this did not create itself. To say the Creator made it just means that it was caused by what caused it. We do not know what caused existence. We know we did not make it. The vastness and complexity of all this, from the tiniest particles of atoms to the distant galaxies turning in space, from the immense energies of the great stars to the mysteries of living cells feeding and growing, overwhelms and astounds our puny brains. What could have done all this? It would require an intelligence far beyond our understanding.

We human beings assign names to it and pretend we know all about it. We say "God" or "Allah" or "Brahman" or "the Great Spirit" or, in my old language, "Kiehtan,". But these are only words. The noises we make to refer to something we truly know nothing about. The myths of human religions inescapably reduce that power or intelligence to terms we can comprehend. So we have made our Creator small enough to fit our small minds. And then we get arrogant about these concepts. We argue and even go to war over them, proclaiming the others' ill intentions and the falsehood of their beliefs.

You see, for us it is our awareness that is so crucial in all that. We might have greater longevity as a mountain or a rock or a grain of sand, even as an old oak tree. But our awareness would be very limited. As it is we can contemplate how our bodies are functioning, what is going on in our minds, and give attention to the feelings in our hearts. If we are really attentive we can sometimes seem to connect with spirits that inhabit all Creation. But that attention is not of our rational faculties, our logical thinking. We devise instruments that enable us to study and learn about the worlds about us, above us, and within us, and our awareness expands on many levels.

What a precious gift is this awareness, and how little do we utilize and honor it through the moments and hours of our days!

This, then, is what it means to walk in a sacred manner. Making every footstep upon the earth a prayer means to attend each moment, each thought and deed, with enhanced awareness. If we are truly alive and attentive we will consider every step carefully, we will be thoughtful of our surroundings, we will make our choices considering the past, all we have learned, and with a vision for the future, while alert and heedful of all the relationships we affect with our present step. In this way, we are mindful of making a path through the world that our children and their children and many generations yet unborn can follow in safety and happiness.

So to make every step a prayer is to be conscious of all our actions. It means to greet ourselves and all around us and recognize our relationship. Relationship is at the essence of the teaching, as is equality and the recognition of the sacredness of all things.

Awareness means giving our attention. Being attentive. When we are attentive our minds are open. We are not concerned with our thoughts and ideas and beliefs. We are not judging. We are not comparing. We are listening and observing. If we have no judgements, no comparisons, no theories, no attitudes, no needs or desires, perhaps then we can catch some perception of what really is. Only then is it possible to confront the truth. When we observe reality uncolored by our preconceived notions, opinions, our ideas and feelings about it, we are open to true learning and growth. We can interact with reality in a natural, balanced way.

Reality, after all, can only be found in this moment. The past is not real, it is a memory and a story, dependent on the limitations of our memories and the viewpoints of the recorders. The future is uncertain and unreal, a conjecture. The only reality is right now. The more we pay attention to what is in this moment the more we are grounded in reality.

Most of the great wisdom traditions of the world teach that the chief function and purpose of a human being is to be aware, to grow in awareness, to learn and grow in learning throughout life. Perhaps Creation has led us to the evolution of our thinking minds for a purpose. The fact that we have such an idea and respond to such an idea of purpose is one reason for believing it may be so. That is why from the moment we are born one of the most prominent traits we immediately display is curiosity. We are curious far beyond what we require for mere survival. We begin at once to learn about our world, and if we are to fulfil our humanity, our Original Instructions, we should never stop.

The awareness we have as adults is colored and conditioned and distorted by the cultures that have educated and impressed themselves upon our consciousness. When we are still babies our learning and impressions of the world around us are still relatively free of this conditioning and education of the culture, but it begins very early. In the very earliest days of life we see things more as they truly are because we have no pre-existing ideas about them.

Watch a small baby examining her environment. The expression on her face is generally calm, relaxed, and curious. She reaches out confidently to explore it. We must be careful there is nothing dangerous within her reach, because she has no terror, holds no taboos about anything. It is all there to be discovered. How it looks, how it feels, how it tastes, if it moves, if it can be lifted, if it can be thrown, and so on. There is no idea in the baby of ownership or possession. All the world around her is her toy. She wants to learn how to relate to it. She knows with an inner knowledge that her reason for being is simply to enjoy, to play, to have fun.

So she seeks to find out how anything can best be utilized for her enjoyment. Including all the people who come to her.

Look into the eyes of an infant, before she has become wary by our fears and anxieties. She will return your look quite calmly, studying you. Absorbing your being. Often you may become aware of a deep connection being made, something beyond the physical awareness, beyond the simple curiosity of two intelligences, beyond the tender feelings naturally inspired by the innocence and sweetness of a tiny human being. The kind of connection that is deeper than the words we have to describe or explain it. The kind of connection we only suggest when we name it spiritual.

There is a new and pure bundle of awareness there, lately arrived from a conception initiated by powerful and little understood forces that drove our parents together for the purpose of bringing us to this life. In this attentive state we may for perhaps only an instant, sense and share a recognition of each other. Two equal beings coming from mystery into more mystery. Though we have grown larger and coarser and explored perhaps much of this world, we know our spiritual understanding is not greater than that of this tiny being so fresh from the Creation. If you should be moved to acknowledge that recognition and appreciate that connection with a smile, the baby will usually affirm her gladness for your affirmation with a smile. Extend a finger and she will probably grasp it and confirm your connection.

We are set out on mysterious journeys through this life, and such a moment of connection may serve to refresh the knowledge that was inborn in all of us: that we need each other. The Original Instructions of human beings remind us that we are social creatures. We became human, became homo sapiens, the thinking hominid, by coming close to each other. By meeting each other as equal beings, by communicating and by cooperating.

To do this we have to learn to listen to each other. There is no communication if you are only trying to express yourself. We must also listen to one another. We need to be capable of stilling our own expression and only be attentive. To silently absorb the other's meaning and being. To be still and focus on our awareness of the other.

In this way the art of communication develops. We study each other for expressions of face and body, and these become a language. We make sounds, meaning something by them, and study what the other means to signify, then imitate and confirm our connection and understanding. So verbal language develops and meaning, concepts, ideas formulate and fill our minds.

Just for this we need each other. Only by communication can we become fully human and set out on the path of understanding, following the Original Instructions. We continue to need each other intellectually, to absorb new knowledge, and as corrective to what we have learned. It is easy to be mistaken when the sources of our knowledge are limited. Falsehood so quickly infests our processes like a virus in the computer if we shut down our connections, our awareness of the other and the correctives of communication. Fot instance, our relationships get snarled, tangled in misapprehension and fantasy, to the extent that we do not communicate our thoughts and perceptions, our sensations and emotions, our desires and fears to each other. When we hear the stories of brothers and sisters it is surprising that they come from the same family, because their perceptions and memories are so different.

So this awareness is very important on a mental level. It has been said that you shall know the truth and that will make you free. But the truth, of course, is not only in ideas, in words and languages of the mind. The truth, other truths, are found in the silent language of the body, of the heart, and of the spirit.

Energy flows where attention goes. Our elders often told the story of the two wolves that battle for our consciousness. One wolf assures us that Creation has sent us there for a purpose, to use our gift of life in the best way, to be happy and hearty and helpful, to give something special back to the world in gratitude. This wolf is there to encourage us and give us strength when we feel discouraged and without power. The other wolf is complaining, "It's too much, you'll never achieve what you seek, you'll never have enough, its hopeless." The first wolf says, "Creation gave you everything you need, be grateful, be happy, but don't give up, reach out to others, support each other, the game is interesting and fun." The other wolf says, "Don't listen to that, just grab what you can and be ready to defend yourself, because no one cares about you – do them before they do you."

So back and forth it goes in our minds, each wolf in a battle for our consciousness, for our lives. And when you ask the elders which wolf will win, they tell you, "The one you feed."

Energy goes where attention flows. This is also an ancient teaching of Huna, wisdom of the indigenous people of Hawaii. By placing focused attention on your senses you can achieve vastly increased sensitivity, and sensual pleasure is greatly magnified with concentrated awareness of the senses. Remarkable physical healing is often produced by concentrating the energies of attention on specific bodily areas of sickness or injury, and sensual pleasure is greatly magnified with concentrated awareness of the senses. If we put our attention on negative thoughts and feelings they will be sure to increase, and conversely when we focus our attention on positive thoughts and feelings we will magnify them.

What we must realize is that this gift of awareness is a great power which comes with the instruction that it is possible and desirable for us to control it consciously. We have been given this faculty of choice which makes human beings more powerful, more creative, and potentially more dangerous than all the other creatures. If we are giving our attention to negative thoughts that will distort our consciousness of reality in that direction. Our thoughts will be darkened with pessimism and our feelings with depression.

People caught in that negative attitude are likely to believe they are looking at the world realistically, while the optimists, idealists and utopians are seeing through wishful rose-colored glasses. But if you are not putting attention on negative thoughts and feelings you can have a much larger view of reality. Putting attention instead on positive thoughts and feelings brings us into balance again. Focussing on health tends to heal us.

There can be times, when we may perhaps become unaware of negativity that has been pushed out of our consciousness but remains at deeper levels where it affects what we may say or do, then it can be good to put our attention on our negative thoughts and feelings, in order to bring them to light, to express and thereby expunge them. Yet it is best not to dwell there too long, not to take our selves and our troubles too seriously, to understand that nothing is forever and the reality of this moment is we are alive and are equipped with all we need to seize the day and make the most of the gift of life.

Our world is overflowing with negativity at every moment. It is we human beings, because we are not following our Original Instructions, that have flooded ourselves in violence, oppression, injustice, destruction, terror and grief. To listen to news of the world and read it in the papers is to become overwhelmed by the enormity of man's inhumanity and to be either enraged or numbed, or sunk in hopelessness. In those states we will effect no positive change. Numbness, hopelessness simply paralyze us, and rage causes us to react emotionally without clear and rational consideration.

We must recognize not only the power of positive thinking, but also the power of negative thinking, and use that power only in a controlled and considered way. A suggestion has been put forward, and I highly endorse it, to make a strong commitment to ourselves and to Creation never to give any attention to our negative thoughts and feelings except at certain agreed upon times for the purpose of uncovering and discharging the negative feelings. Then, with our minds more objective, relaxed and clear, we will make better plans and decisions.

Awareness feeds our lives. Directing our awareness feeds our brains. We absorb new data and our minds expand. With an active mind that continually grows we rejuvenate ourselves, body and mind. Our natural curiosity keeps us alert and vibrant.

Things to think about: What are you aware of right now? Close your eyes. What do you hear? What do you remember seeing before you closed your eyes? Be aware of your breathing, of your heart beat and pulse. Where are you now in your journey? Where do you want to go? What do you want to learn? If you want to stay young in heart and mind, pay attention, ask questions, investigate, contemplate. Learn something new, take up a new course of study, probe your interests, follow them, follow your wonder.

Travelling with elders I was always surprised by the extent of their awareness of what was going on around them. Sometimes they would comment on an occurence or a relationship in some place and utterly different culture that I had no idea they would notice, but their comments always showed a remarkable insight that hanged the perspetions of others. Sometimes they did not comment, but I could see and read in their eyes that they had noticed things others had not.

When we consider what may be true from a spiritual viewpoint, we find a different understanding from that which we have confined to our limited physical situation and the tiny purview of our minds and hearts. When we can expand our attention beyond our own selves, our individual needs and desires, even beyond our loved ones, our community, our people, beyond our fellow creatures and all of life, beyond the earth, beyond the circles of the stars, when we pay attention to the entire cosmos as the mind of Creation, then we are seeing in a sacred manner the spirit with which we are one.

This is the deep truth. The Reality that all is well in Creation.

While I plan all I must do today the languid ducks
Just cruise the moment, letting northlands wait:
When the time comes they will be on their way.
Meanwhile mice and squirrels and chipmunks rustle
The dry leaves. In the larger pond below the hill
Mother beaver stirs her mate, "It's half-past
April, time to get busy, the house is a wreck,
The children are famished, the dam leaks,
The otters already out and scouring the pond."
Now the drone of a single plane slices the sky
Like a buzz-saw, reminding both of us
Of the human world beyond that feeds and grows
On its own toxicity, the hunger of its maw
Seeking to swallow every forest, all
Our ash and oak and hemlock, every maple,
Hickory, birch and beech, pine and cedar,
The mice, chipmunks, squirrels, rabbits, deer,
Wildcat, wolf, coyote, moose, raccoon,
Skunk and porcupine, beaver, badger, possum,
Scurrying quail, grouse, turkey and pheasant,
Hawks, eagles, falcons, buzzards keeping watch.
Where will we all go? How should there be life
When April returns but the forest is no more?
I want to tell that pilot up there, all the people
Raging the roads of sky and land, come back,
You won't find it anywhere that you are going:
Not peace, nor love, nor freedom, nor joy, nor life –
Nothing your soul requires is there to be found,
Only more search and stress and never April.
Come instead to the woods and follow your love.

                    (Excerpt from "April in our Woods" – 2005)

5. HUMOR: PLAYFULNESS

In preparing to write this section I have written several words as possible titles. "Joy", "Humor", Fun", "Pleasure", Happiness", "Laughter", "Playfulness". Each with its own separate meaning belongs in this category somehow. Perhaps you can just think of all of them as you listen.

The elders didn't talk about play or playfulness as such. But they lived them. The wisest teachers were always playful and had a lively and irrepressible sense of humor that never quit. Humor is playing with the world, with how things appear to us. The deepest wisdom sees humor everywhere, even in tragedy. It is enlarging our consciousness to a cosmic level where everything is, to our limited conditioning, a bit strange and peculiar, odd and funny.

We human beings all love dolphins and otters. They touch our hearts. Why? It is their playfulness. They are not forever bent upon the grim task of survival. They take time, indeed a great deal of their time, to have fun. We love to watch them sporting about, relishing the sheer joy of movement, of energy and life. And enjoying each other, engaging each other sportively. We are delighted to watch monkeys at play, or the swallows swooping endlessly after one another over our heads.

It seems we have this instruction. It is very human to play, to laugh, to joy in our existence. To have fun, as do the dolphins and the otters and the monkeys and other animals. The eagle and the hawk, the sea gull and the pelican may be engaged in examining their realms for food, but does it not seem they are also relishing their own movements, feeling the currents of air, the lift and pull of the wind, as they soar and wheel and dive through the sky? Likewise the wolves and foxes and the great cats appear to enjoy the hunt, the exercise of their senses and their wit, as well as of their supple bodies. Do the birds sing only for practical purposes, or are they also deriving pleasure from the melodies, the tones and the variations of their songs? Does the hummingbird enjoy the beauty of his flight, the colors of flowers that attract him, and the sweetness of the nectar?

If it seems so to us, it must be that we have this instruction built into our being, to our genes, through our DNA. We want pleasure. We want to be happy. We can feel that experiencing pleasure is one part of attaining that happiness. There are other parts, of course. Or perhaps we might say there are many kinds of pleasure. The pleasure of feeling love. The pleasure of giving. The pleasure of contemplating beauty. The pleasure of creating. The pleasure of learning, of assimilating knowledge, of deducing and solving puzzles, of exploring, of having new insights, of finding meaning.

53

For part of every year Ellika, my wife and partner in all things, and I live in her very small house in the free haven of Christiania in Copenhagen, part of a community of families whose small houses group about a playground and day-care house for small children. At every meal, breakfast to dinner, we can sit at table and watch through the window the children playing – the small ones during the day, and later the older ones coming from school. Every moment they are not eating or sleeping they are playing. Their energy is immense, explosive, concentrated, and, to us old folks, seemingly inexhaustible.

Let us invite you there now to have a good example before us as we discuss play and humor. It's that little Swedish red house at the southeast corner of the playground. Come on in, we'll put on some tea and coffee and watch the small human comedy outside our big window.

What a joy it is to watch them. Their exuberance and imagination bursts through them and darts everywhere – like the swallows overhead. We are absorbed, vicariously playing their games which they invent as they go. We recall our own childhoods and what it was like then to live in a world where our main responsibility was to our play. Play was the instruction from Creation by which we lived. We devoted ourselves to it happily, with all our attention, with all our wit and knowledge. Through it we learned about relating with others of our kind and developed qualities of leadership and cooperation while also discovering what it means to hurt and be hurt by our peers.

It seems that playfulness, the art of play, was one of our very first instructions. In growing out of childhood we as adults have assumed a theory that all that play was only to grow through, to teach us skills for life. Once we achieved those skills we were supposed to set aside play for serious work. In my opinion that is a mistake. I cannot think of any serious endeavor that human beings engage in that would not be done better employing our playfulness. Play is the essence of creativity.

Closely allied to play is curiosity, which we also notice in newborns from the very beginning. Babies stare long at new things, new faces. And then they want to explore them. They touch, feel, hold, taste, lift if they can, pull and push and throw. They are playing and they are learning, gaining knowledge and understanding. That curiosity, that exploration, that learning is one of our built-in instructions. And we do not outgrow it. It will continue through our lives, making them richer and more meaningful – more pleasurable.

Another human characteristic we can notice, if we are paying attention to our newborns, is a development of tenderness, a pleasure in human touch, softness, warmth, caress. Very early the child who is lovingly touched learns to touch, to hug and to kiss, and enjoys both the giving and the receiving. This becomes an expression of the sentiment of caring which the child feels for those who care for her. Soon it may be seen that if the mother or grandparent or brother or anyone close to the child displays distress or sadness, the child will hug and caress that person and show concern for his feelings. This bond of love and caring grows from infancy if not discouraged and becomes stronger with advancing years. It is an essentially human trait, one of our most important instructions, if not the most important.

One other important human characteristic that begins to develop in childhood is that of creativity. When we learn to produce sounds with our vocal chords we start to sing. Once we learn to manipulate things with our hands we begin to make things. When we learn to stand and walk we begin to dance. When we learn to appreciate stories that we are told, we begin to make up our own. Creativity is inborn in all of us, though we each tend to develop different expressions of it. Our creativity proceeds from the application of our knowledge and intelligence through our physical prowess by means of our playfulness. Artists and other creative people recognize the origins of their work in play. Not only children but also adults need to be aware that we are all creative and that therefore playfulness is essential to all we do.

Many of our creation stories suggest the genesis of existence out of play. The Creator Spirit wants something to do and begins to play. Creation begins to sing, and through that singing are born the stars, sun, moon and earth. From that singing the mountains rise, the waters fill the rivers, lakes, and the seas, and the seeds of living things begin to move in earth and water. Like our own creativity that imitates it, Creation arises and continues through playfulness. The energies all about us, bursting from the seeds, exploding through leaf and flower and fruit, dancing the dances of nourishment and procreation, are alive with play.

As the play gets more complex in the progress of evolution, simple life that procreates through division develops a new game, the game of sex. With this new game life can get much more complicated, develop in so many fascinating ways. In the more complicated species, in monkeys for instance, in dolphins, and in human beings we see clearly that this game, this dance of sex, is informed and advanced by play and an intense sensation of pleasure.

I will never forget my first view of freshwater dolphins through the glass in the San Francisco aquarium where we could watch them below the surface of the water. They played and played with each other. They raced and turned and dove, came together, caressed and parted, in a long, slow, beautiful ballet. I stood watching, fascinated, for a long time before I noticed that as they came together he slipped his penis into her vagina for just a moment before they split, swam away from each other, and then around and together again. It was a dance of sex! The loveliest dance I had ever seen. And like the best human sexual encounters it was, considerate, tender, playful, and amazingly creative.

That scene has returned to me often over the ensuing forty years, causing me to contemplate the role of pleasure in the lives of us mammals. Modern medicine has been doing a lot of research into endorphins and serotonin, chemical producers of pleasure in our bodies. I don't choose to go into that in depth here. I only want to say it seems to me that Creation has gone to great endeavor to install the pleasure sense in us. And since I believe that everything has a purpose in Creation, it's probably a good idea to pay attention to pleasure.

I realize that all pleasure is not equally good, safe, healthy, and creative. Human beings have in their dark history devised many evil, cruel, hurtful and destructive "pleasures". These, however, are aberrations, not natural human pleasures. The minds that enjoyed them were twisted and hurt by horrific experiences.

We would be wise to posit as the norm for human nature the natures of those who were raised in a human way. The human way of child raising, as our Original Instructions guide us, is with a watchful attention, the provision not only of safety, nourishment, and a comfortable environment, but also warm and tender caressing and expression of love and approval. Beyond that the instruction is not to interfere with the child's freedom to explore and discover, except to prevent injury to themselves or others, to allow full expression in play. No child raised in such a manner will ever find pleasure in hurting other creatures. When they destroy things it is not out of malice, but out of the same curiosity and exploration through which they are learning about the world, and because they have no cause to have the same valuation of those things as we adults do.

Among the many occupations I have had in my long lifetime I have often been a teacher of the young of all ages, and for one year my former wife and I made a day care center in our home. So I have observed children at play extensively and often participated in it with them. Most children play and interact imaginatively with one another. Cooperation is natural to all human beings – it is fundamental to what made us human in the first place. When children are not cooperating, when they become aggressive and seek to dominate, injure, or punish other children, you understand that at home they have experienced domination, abuse, and punishment. And so at the end of the day when the parents came for their offspring, we could always recognize and correlate what we observed with the relations we saw between parent and child. The children who were generally friendly, cooperative, and imaginative, discovering fun with others, had sunny dispositions and laughed a lot, always had parents who always had warm, friendly relations with relaxed parents who had a good sense of humor. The difficult aggressive children had at least one parent who was rigid and judgmental and punitive.

We learned that play and humor are the best ways to reach and be close to all children. The best way to teach and to counsel children is to engage them in play. With angry and aggressive children it is often necessary to restrain them from destructive behavior, while allowing them to vent their anger and hostility against you. It is important then to keep a light and friendly tone and not react harshly or with anger. Not always easy, as aggression and anger will probably stir up our own feelings (which later we may need to pay attention to with a friend's support). While I am restraining a child in as gentle but firm way as I can, I am telling myself the child does not really want to be doing this and would much rather be playing and having fun, but does not know how to deal with those powerful emotions, which my restraining helps to bring out. Probably the child will jump at an opportunity for humor eventually, perhaps at my expense, which I will encourage and play with.

There is a section of the <u>Reader's Digest</u>, "Laughter is the Best Medicine". And we know that's true, no doubt about it. Perhaps you have heard the story of how <u>Saturday Review</u> editor Norman Cousins cured himself of a fatal disease his doctors thought incurable by immersing himself in the irresistible hilarity of films by such as the Marx Brothers, Charlie Chaplin and Buster Keaton. I don't find that at all hard to believe. Such clowns have sent me to the floor in helpless spasms of howling laughter until my body ached with it, and it's hard for me to imagine any sickness being able to reside among such conditions.

Laughter is a very special expression of extreme joy that at its most intense can grasp our whole being, body, mind, heart and soul, and shake it until we weep. However extreme the experience we do not regret it but rejoice in the vitality of it and the cleansing for a moment of our negativity, our sadness, our anxiety, our irritation, our boredom, our confusion. For that moment we are touched and filled with the spirit of life itself, the energy of Creation.

Watch those children in the playground. They cannot contain their laughter. It erupts from them periodically. Sometimes they abandon all attempts to continue and give themselves over to it entirely rolling on the ground in screaming glee.

Someone made a study of children and found that the average five year old laughs 400 times a day (or was it that four year olds laugh 500 times a day? No matter. It's a lot). Can you imagine yourself laughing four or five hundred times a day? I'm a pretty good laugher, but that is beyond me. But perhaps we both laughed like that every day when we were small.

What happened? Oh, life, you know, that serious business. And this culture we all struggle through is not a lot of fun. They don't help you to laugh in school. It's discouraged in class and in the halls as well. "Quiet down, children. This is no laughing matter."

Then we get a job. Not a lot of giggles there either. You might get married, have children, very serious propositions. The older you get the more serious you're supposed to be. You get sick and everyone gets gloomy. When you die they get to wear black and be truly solemn.

When I was a teenager my stepfather tried to help me with a career choice by getting me appointments at advertising firms that were clients of his. A natural idea for a boy handy with language. Only I didn't want to write advertising copy. I wrote poetry, and thought about perhaps writing plays or novels. But as a dutiful son I went and was appalled by the frenetic sense of tension and anxiety in those agencies and mystified by their pride in their foolish slogans. I told my stepfather I didn't think I would enjoy that line of work.

"Enjoy?" my stepfather exclaimed, "Do you think I <u>enjoy</u> my work?"

What a shock! The realities of the business world came home to me for the first time. It had never occurred to me that he might be suffering through five days of joyless toil all week in order to have the right to putter in the garden on the other two days and forget his cheerless life in alcohol every night.

It was just too sad to imagine trading away your life, giving up on fun for a nice house with a garden and two cars in the garage. For perhaps a two week vacation every year which might be fun if you haven't forgotten how to have it, and laughter only induced by TV. What poverty, to have one's fun reduced to being a spectator of professional sports!

The English philosopher John Locke said everyone has a natural right to "Life, liberty, and property." Quite British, eighteenth century. The American Thomas Jefferson took the idea into his "Declaration of Independence", but changed it to "Life, liberty and the pursuit of happiness." Alexander Hamilton would probably have preferred "property". It doesn't matter. American culture gives lip service to Jefferson, but it is Hamilton it follows. Happiness, through all that the culture teaches, in its schools and through its media and politics, is equated with property. Material wealth. If you get it you will be happy, fulfilled, appreciated, accepted and loved. If you don't you won't.

The whole culture, with America as its prime exponent and example, believes and follows this canon. The only problem is that it isn't true. And following that American dream not only devastates the planet, rendering it less and less habitable, it also betrays its own end, creating stress and misery instead of happiness.

We started out happy – most of us. Remember? Five hundred laughs a day! Look at them running around the playground out there. That was us when we were that size. I ask again, what happened? Where is the fun in your life now? It's worth thinking about. This is the only life you get, and it's slipping away. Faster and faster as you get older, believe me. How can you increase the fun you have or if you have none at all, how can you get it into your life?

First, you probably need to let go of whatever stresses you. Will you look at that? If you are like most people today you may carry a load of stress. As a counselor I hear this all the time. "I'm so stressed. There's not enough time. Too much to do. Constant pressure…" It's the major symptom of modern society – stress.

You may be bedeviled with worries. Is that so? If it is, they are stealing your life. Think about that. Perhaps it should be a priority – letting go of stress and worry. What is really important to you? Is it happiness – yours and that of those you love? If that is what is important, what is in the way of your happiness? What keeps you from having fun and silences your laughter?

There are ways to get rid of stress and worry. That is not the province of this book. You can find that help if you make it your priority and search for it. I only raise the question because playfulness and laughter are part of our Original Instructions that you may wish to consider.

I can tell you one way to recover your playfulness and laughter. Find yourself a very young newborn of any kind, a puppy or a kitten perhaps. Get close. Down at their level. Watch her play. Reach out – does she want to engage you? Can you remember playing with a baby animal when you were a child? Get into it. Let yourself laugh, it's okay.

Now graduate to a human baby. Begin with a young infant – it's easy to be silly with a very young one, and the games you devise together are simple. You are learning together, learning each other, building a relationship by playing. Graduate yourself to older infants – get down to their level and crawl with them. When they have an object of play, follow that. When not, take the lead and invent a game. Get physical. Get silly. Forget you are a grown-up. If the baby pushes you, fall over helplessly. She has possibly never been able to push over an adult and will find it hilarious. Finally she gets to have power! Finally a big person who knows how to play and is willing to be with just her. Laugh along with her. A lot.

Keep going up the age scale. Find a toddler, see what her play is about and enter it whole-heartedly. (I hope you have friends with small children if you don't have your own. Offer some baby-sitting, they will be grateful.) It keeps getting more of a stretch as the children get older. Hang out at a day-care, a pre-school, a kindergarten. Don't bring your own ideas of what to do. You are learning here. These are your teachers. They are the experts in play. It's their job, what they do during every waking moment, and they are good at it. You were once, too, and it's still there inside you if you allow it. Give up any idea about dignity or propriety or cleverness, just be funny, be stupid, be foolish, be a clown. When they laugh you are onto something. Don't forget to laugh too.

Keep advancing your play through older children, following their games. But still don't try to win them all. Be a little bit klutzy, trip and fall a lot, let yourself get tackled, tickled, mauled. Give them a rare opportunity to be really powerful and lord it over an adult. When you are killed, die gloriously, with overblown melodrama. When you are chased, let yourself be caught often. When you chase, almost catch your victim who once more manages a last second escape. Keep laughing, howling, squealing. Go past the point of exhaustion until you can't go any further. Then sit down and laugh.

Perhaps you can find an adult friend with whom you can trade stories about your childhoods and talk about how it feels to relive and recover some of that lost playfulness. If you have a circle, a close community, or you can bring parents together for a support group; suggest having a play day with the children.

In our community, while our children were growing, we mandated a play day once a month. It was the most important day of the month for everyone, adult and child, and attendance was compulsory. We all went to some park or recreation area, took a picnic, and played together all day in the ways I have just described. It was as good for the grown-ups as for the young people. Now they are all grown and gone we elders have to travel to find communities with children. Or live, as we do here, on the side of a playground and day-care. In our camps we always designate one play day a week where all the adults get to play with all the children.

What does Creation want? I keep asking this question, all my life. Perhaps it's the most important question for us all. It is for me. Asking who I am seems essential, and the most certain of all possible answers is that I am a part of Creation. An essential part. What part is not essential? So when I seek to know what I am to do, how I am to live, I must return to the understanding that, solitary as I might often seem to myself, that is illusion. I am not alone. I am a relative to all that is. I am in fact at one with Creation.

If I am to know what to do I must know what I want. Since I am one with Creation, I must ask what it is that Creation wants. Being part of Creation the answer must at least in part lie within me. But Creation is vast, and the answer must be everywhere else. What is Creation doing?

It is moving, expanding. Also, with life, becoming more complex and more intelligent. The whole of Creation is more intelligent than foolish little human life, but we are part of it. So perhaps its movement, its expansion includes expanding awareness. I feel that desire for expanded awareness in me, so probably that's at least a part of it.

I also respond to the old stories that say Creation arose out of play. And Creation is continuing around us, through burgeoning life here, and out in the expanses of the universe. Play is going on everywhere. See the winds playing with the clouds, with the waves, with the leaves in the trees, with the grass, with my hair. See the butterflies and hummingbirds at play in the flowers. See the cat playing with her prey. See the swallows playing with each other, the dolphins, the otters, the monkeys. And watch the cubs, the pups, the kits, and our own children.

The children have a clear wisdom fresh from Creation. Life is for having fun. The world is a playground. When we play we are following the same Original Instructions as all life follows.

When we weep we are healing our hearts, when we laugh we are expanding into the cosmic/comic mind of Creation.

People must suffer hard times in order to endure. The unfailing humor of the people does the best for getting through hard times. Black Elk said the people need laughter in these times, and that was the reason for some ceremonies. The tradition of the sacred clowns is strong among many ancient cultures, not only among our people but also around the world. The clowns dress and paint themselves in ridiculous ways that make you laugh just by looking at them. Then they do stupid and crazy things, imitating and exaggerating ordinary actions of people to reflect how funny we really all are. Children all over the world are convulsed with screaming hilarity by the antics of clowns, and we adults love them too, though our dignity may restrain us a bit more.

My elder and very dear friend John Fire, Lame Deer, was a holy man and also a man of irrepressible humor. At one point in his career he had been a professional rodeo clown. I'm sorry that was before I knew him (he was 40 years my senior), and I can only imagine his antics then as I saw them often later.

An audience, large or small, would set off a twinkle in his eye that I came to know presaged some comic commentary. Once we stood watching a yogi guide a large crowd at an outdoor festival in Boulder, Colorado. The guru told people to hold their hands over their heads and breathe in. Everyone did that. He told them to close one nostril with a finger and breathe out, then do the same with the other nostril. They did.

Lame Deer watched all the exercises until they were over and the yogi left the stage. I had seen the gleam in John's eye and knew his brain was cooking up something, so I wasn't surprised when he leaped on the stage. There was a murmur as the crowd recognized the well-known medicine man. He told the audience to put their right arms straight forward from their shoulders. They did. He told them to bend their arms at the elbow, and they did. He said to spread their fingers wide apart. Everyone obeyed. He asked that they now copy his movements, which they carefully did as he slowly brought his hand to his face, applied the end of his thumb to the end of his nose, and wiggled his fingers at them all. He sprang from the stage and rejoined me as the crowd behind him roared with laughter. Lame Deer's yoga was a hit!

We were often together at events and asked to give talks or be on panels. I was probably invited out of courtesy as a rare representative of an eastern tribe in the west. When one of these events was over, everyone went their own ways leaving us to figure out what to do for the night in a strange town. Lame Deer turned to me.

"Well, Medicine Story, we are a couple of holy men on our own now," he said.

"Okay," I responded doubtfully, happy to be considered a spiritual companion to my elder, but already preparing myself for the punch line.

"Okay, let's go and find us a couple of holy women," he twinkled.

There was one man Lame Deer was always delighted to see appear at our Indian gatherings – old Henry Knockwood, Mic Mac from Nova Scotia.

"Henry, I'm so glad you came," Lame Deer would greet him. "It makes me look good because you're the only man in the world uglier than I am!"

In a phrase he made fun of himself and Henry affectionately and of all human attitudes about good looks. In truth both men had faces as beautiful as the Badlands or the jagged rocks of Cape Breton.

Indians by ourselves are always joking and laughing, but that is often subdued when non-Indians are there. Perhaps we aren't sure how non-Indians will take our humor. Laughter may be shared with a quick glance but an otherwise straight face.

One time my friend Don McCloud was preparing salmon in traditional northwestern style for cooking at an open fire. As we stood by talking a professorial looking white man came up to watch and immediately took out a notebook and began to write. Evidently he was interested in native "secrets" of broiling salmon. Don noted this and began to make his actions slower and more deliberate, pausing while the man entered in his notes whatever herb or spice Don applied to the fish. Don fit the fish onto sticks then held each one up before him and with a ritual flourish pretended, quite realistically to spit all over both sides of each fish.

All the native men had to turn quickly away to hide their barely contained mirth as the note-taker, with widened eyes wrote furiously in his little book!

My colleague Slow Turtle once introduced me, for a talk I was to give, with about twenty minutes of roasting and raillery at my expense that was hilarious. Always a comedian, he was, as they say, "on a roll," improvising brilliantly. It was hard to get serious enough for my talk, but my wife said later that she then saw more clearly than ever the depth of my friend's love for me.

We used to perform a sweat lodge ceremony together in one of the Connecticut prisons one morning a month, then in the afternoon lead a circle in another nearby prison. After the sweat we were both depleted and exhausted and could hardly keep our heads up, so we would take turns speaking and sleeping through the other's speech.

"Don't talk too long," he would tell me, "I'm an old man."

"Don't sleep too long," I would answer, "I'm older than you!"

Well, the talk is about humor, so maybe we ought to have a few more laughs now.

The other day I was with a group of old guys sitting at the local diner. Great place for absorbing some laconic country humor. Someone remarked upon another man's new white socks.

"You been shopping, eh?"

"Ayuh."

"Buy anything besides socks?"

"Nope. Didn't want to overheat the economy."

Someone mentioned a young preacher who was newly assigned to an Indian community back here whose first job was to perform a funeral for the previous preacher, whom no one had liked. He had been solitary and aloof and stern, and had seemed to get even more sour after the death of his old brother. Since the young preacher had not known this man he asked the group gathered about the grave if there was someone who might say a few words of eulogy. The people glanced at each other, but no one moved.

"Come, you all knew this man, someone must be able to say a few good words about him."

No one stirred.

"There must be someone who can say something good about him, speak up."

Just then someone coughed, trying to keep from laughing on this solemn occasion. Everyone looked at him. The minister said, "Yes? What can you tell us about him?"

The man looked about him, No one was going to help him out of this.

"Well," he said, "his brother was worse."

They told about a woman who was unsatisfied with her husband's waning sexual interest so she went to a medicine man for love medicine. He gave her a vial of liquid and told her one drop in the old fellow's soup would be enough.

"How did it go?" her neighbor asked her later.

"It worked fine," the woman said. When Henry wasn't looking I put three drops in his soup that night."

"Three drops?"

"I figured he was a really tough case. "

"So what happened?"

"After he ate the soup he pulled me up, tore off my clothes and made love to me right there on the table."

"Wow!"

"It was wonderful, but, poor Henry, he can't ever show his face in that restaurant again!"

An old Indian cowboy came into the bar and sat beside an attractive blonde woman. She looked at him curiously, because he was quite evidently Indian but also wore a typical cowboy garb.

"Are you a real cowboy?" she asked.

"Yes, ma'am. I'm all day on my horse, herding them critters, roping, tying branding, everything. I guess you could say I'm a real cowboy. What about yourself?"

"Well, I'm a lesbian. I wake up every morning thinking about women, think about women when I shower and have breakfast and all through the day, and at night I dream about women. Yup, I'm a lesbian, all right."

Later another man came in the bar and asked the old Indian the same question.

"Are you a real cowboy?"

"Well, I used to think so, but I just found out I'm a lesbian."

Les, the bartender, said an old man came into the bar one night and asked for a glass of whisky and two drops of water. Les is used to all kinds of unusual drink orders, but as he served the old man he inquired about this one. "Why only two drops of water?" The old man answered, "I'm 78 years old and at my age I can still hold my liquor - but I can't say as much for my water."

And everyone always loves the story of the two Lakota boys who were out of work and had no food, so since they were fasting anyway they decided to make a sweat lodge. When it was ready they crawled in, saying "O metakwe oasin," ("all my relations," in Lakota). Inside they prayed and asked the Creator if some food might not be sent their way, as they were getting a bit weak from fasting. They crawled out again, saying, in traditional fashion, "O mitwake oasin," – "All my Relations."

Just then they saw a very large turtle crawling by. They thanked Creator, grabbed up the turtle, took him inside their new government community center, put it into the microwave oven, turned it on and sat down to wait. In ten minutes the bell rang, the door opened, and the turtle crawled out saying "O mitwake oasin."

Things to think about: Are you serious? Does that help? Anything you can not laugh about? Anything too hurtful to laugh at? Anything too sacred to be funny? Could you make a joke about something that seems truly terrible? Can you laugh at yourself?

Thirty years ago, on the Spokane Reservation, I heard a story I still tell. It was a time when young people were beginning to seek and learn their old ceremonies. A group of young men were being introduced to the mysteries of the sweat lodge. They had heard a lot of things about the power of the lodge, about visions that could occur, about spirits that might be present. The prospect of crawling in that little place and sitting in absolute dark was pretty terrifying. Inside they were so crowded they had to draw up their knees and were unable to move. As the heat increased and the leader prayed in the old language, one young man began to lose sensation in his right leg. In a panic he thought some spirit wanted to invade him. In the dark he leaned over and bit his right knee. No feeling at all. Now he was really terrified, but being an Indian was more afraid of showing his fear. After a bit he tried again. Nothing. Dead meat. Not knowing what to do he tried a third time with the same result.

Just then the leader completed the ceremony, opened the door, and they all crawled out. To the boy's relief his leg worked and sensation began to return to it. Standing with the others around the fire he felt the need to say something and hear other reactions.

"Powerful spirits in that lodge, ennit?" he offered tentatively.

"Yeah," said the young man standing next to him, 'one bit me on the knee three times!"

All my elders had a remarkable sense of humor and playfulness. I have mentioned Lame Deer whom I was especially close to and who had actually been a professional rodeo clown, whose outlook was always wickedly skewed and impish.

But it was true in different ways of others like Janet McCloud, Thomas Banyacya, Mad Bear Anderson, Beeman Logan, Madas Sapiel, Senabeh, Joe Sunhawk, and so many others whose humor crept out from behind a seriousness of purpose.

Could it be that everything that is going on in Creation is pure play? Just fun?

COYOTE LOVE

They call me Coyote
Some people that is
I don't know about that
Sometimes I feel like him
But as far as I can tell
I don't know him so well
I call him friend
To be polite
But I keep my eye on him
He's got a reputation

Anyway there I am all alone
Being pretty well connected
My naked skin just an extension
Of soil and rock and grass
Salted with sea, browned
By distant steady silent
Solar explosion
Fondled by erotic breezes
I sense enough of the Unity
To be ready to love without
Need or longing or desperation

Then I hear a cough like a chuckle
Turn and he's right behind me
All innocent and foolish
And I suddenly wonder
If I am he after all
Or just what is real

You only want to hump the world
Says Coyote - well, of course, I say
If flesh is spirit, spirit flesh -
Too deep for me says Coyote
But that's what I always say too
And he trots off laughing his head off
Like it's all just one big joke
I shake my head, giggling like a fool
What can you do?

6. HONESTY

Honesty is a primary value for many people the world over, but is an especially essential teaching in our First Nations of North America. You might think that honesty would be highly regarded in all cultures, but I have learned that this is not so. There have been and are cultures in which lying is a cultivated art and is expected and a good liar is appreciated. I do not think I would care to live in such a society. The one I do inhabit is bad enough in that way. What with false political rhetoric and promises, exaggerated advertising claims, corporate cover-ups, creative book-keeping, governments lying to their people and to other governments, we are already swimming hard to keep from drowning in a sea of mendacity.

It seems to me that dishonesty is initially and basically caused by fear. Now most of the dishonesty we find around us seems to be caused by greed, so now I'm wondering if greed may not also be caused initially by fear. That's an intriguing thought for another conversation, but I want to stick with fear just now.

You may have noticed that elders seem to be more consistently candid in their speech than younger folk. If you haven't felt that, no doubt you will when you yourself attain an advanced age. I know I have often felt that about myself. The older you get, the closer to the end of life you come, the less you are troubled by little fears that clustered about you when you were younger. You see yourself in a longer, larger perspective. It doesn't matter any more what people might think about you or whether you obtain or lose this or that formerly desired goal. The only fear a sensible older person might have concerns diminished health or capacity, and there's no reason not to be honest about that.

Whenever anyone, you or me, is dishonest or hides the truth it is because we are afraid. And life works much better in human society when people are honest. Of course, if what we are afraid of is only that we might hurt their feelings by being candid about their new dress or the food they prepared, it might not be helpful but only unkind to reveal all of what we think. Unless our honest appraisal is extremely important to them, in which case the truth, however it hurts, would be more kind than concealing it.

It is true that some cultures value honesty more than others. There is a story about a rich American who hired an Indian guide to take him hunting in the wilds of Canada. They left the wilderness cabin early in the morning, and in an hour the man exclaimed they must go back because he left his wallet with a lot of money on the table. "Don't worry," the guide said, "there's not a white man around for a hundred miles."

I went to the movies recently and saw a spy film. This was not an adventure fantasy like James Bond, but a very realistic portrayal of the teachings of espionage by the government of the United States. It was an interesting puzzle to sort out the truth within the levels of intrigue. But I quickly realized I do not care to live in a society like this. One in which lies and deception are not just common but are the desiderata of the government. Nothing is to be relied upon, nothing is what it seems, and everyone is masquerading, pretending, and misdirecting. Any means to accomplish the end, which is to defeat the enemy. An enemy, by the way, which has been defined and created by the government itself.

The most necessary ingredient in all human relationship is trust. The more trust there is in a society, a community, a family, the better they function. The less trust there is, the more they break down. The building of trust should be central to our efforts in improving our society, our community, and our relationships. One of the most essential building blocks of trust is honesty. Nothing destroys trust faster than dishonesty and lying.

When I was a young boy I used to contrive to be sick on the first day of April so that I did not have to go to school. To spend a whole day being tricked by little falsehoods gleefully administered by one's friends with a triumphant shout of "April Fool!" was horrible to me. Not being able to trust anything anyone said made me dizzy, disoriented, anxious, a mysterious terror nibbling at my innards that I couuld not reveal. It was especially terrible that I could not trust my teachers or parents or any adults in a world suddenly gone mad. It was supposed to be fun. I preferred the honest woods and the meadow where all was what it appeared to be.

That kind of dishonesty does not arise from fear, I suppose. It is only a game. Perhaps people who feel constrained by the ordinary social needs of honesty get a sense of release on that one day a year when it is socially acceptable to fool one's fellows and convince others of untruths. For myself, I confess I still prefer the woods and the meadows.

I hope it is really clear to you how essential trust is in all relationships, including all of society. When governments lie and hide the truth from the people, we have a sick, destructive and decaying society. When the media fail to report all the important news and withhold information that might tarnish or injure powerful interests, including that of the government, people can have no ability to deal with the reality of their situation. The limits of their power are then defined by those powerful interests. When business can lie about its products or services we are at their mercy. When nations lie about each other's threats, their people are dragged fearfully into war and they see their children slaughtered to defend the interests of others.

It is clear that the United States today, together with its allied democratic nations, fares better in the areas of openness and honesty than many, perhaps most of the rest of the world's nations where the machinations of government are hidden from their people and the world. But secrecy and lies are still far too prevalent and accepted in the inner circles of power in these "enlightened" democracies. To the extent that any people cannot know the truth, they are captive to the control of the power-motivated interests that contrive to conceal the truth.

And it is clear that a lot of dishonesty derives from the desire for wealth or power. Is that also due to fear? I believe so. The teachings of this competitive, individualist society are that not only happiness but the basic worth of human beings depend upon the accumulation of wealth, power, and glory. There is the great fear that without money an individual will be lost and destroyed. He will at least not be a successful human being. He is alone in a dog-eat-dog world that seeks to obliterate him. He must have money, and it's never enough to feel really safe. Even people of great wealth have the feeling they could lose it all and become destitute. So they always want more. And they must buy power to protect their accumulation. For some, their self-worth is contingent on the admiration of others, so they seek glory, renown, fame, prestige. These too may be purchased.

But fear lurks in the heart of all this ambition. So people lie. They lie on their resumés to get jobs. They lie in order to seem more successful and climb higher up the ladder of success. They lie to their stockholders, to their employees, to their competitors, to the Internal Revenue Service. They hire accountants, attorneys, and public relations people to lie for them.

Industries lie about the harmful effects of their activities on the environment or on human health. The alcohol, tobacco, drug, and insurance industries, energy, automobile, travel, real estate, just about any industry we can think of, all regularly engage in lying to mislead and manipulate the public about any harmful results of their operations, products or services. Individuals lie about taking performance enhancing drugs, about sexual proclivities and activities, about their ages, their histories, their health, their state of mind, the state of their relationships, their fears, their fantasies, and even their hopes. It is not only accused criminals who lie. Too often police and prosecutors lie or cover up evidence to convict a person they <u>believe</u> guilty, to have a high rate of convictions and make their jobs more secure.

It's April Fool's Day every day in the ordinary workings of our world. So we are not overly shocked when politicians and corporate executives are caught in lies and manipulations of books and records. We do not deal with them nearly as harshly as we do a kid who has grown up on the streets, a product of abusive homes and institutions, who has learned survival by retailing controlled substances. We expect that the news will all be slanted, revelations in any medium to be only those approved by publishers and producers.

Honesty and integrity are most highly valued in most tribal societies. Certainly I have found this to be true from my own experience everywhere in North America. From the beginning children are treated to stories about trickster "con" artists like Coyote, Iktome, Raven, Lox and others whose words are not to be trusted. They have an "angle," to get unfair advantage, for food, prestige, or sex. We laugh and shake our heads. We would not want to be like that. And anyone who seems to stretch the truth in his own favor, who seems a bit too sharp and shady in his dealings.whose actions belie his stated beliefs, becomes the subject of much gossip and caution in the community.

"Walk your talk," is a phrase much favored by Native people. A hypocrite quickly reveals himself by how he acts and loses the trust of those who know him. Con men must be loners and keep moving. People who live together in community need to be able to trust each other. That's the reason for much continuing mistrust of the non-Indian in our communities. Because from the first contact it has seemed that what these conquerors could not get by force or stealing they would take by guile and cheating. To the people of the First Nations the unilateral breaking by the colonial governments, by the U.S. and Canada, of every treaty is proof enough of the basic dishonesty and untrustworthiness of the non-Indian. When the Indians gave their word both they and their descendants held it sacred. Treaties were never broken from the Indian side. From the other side, none were kept.

This situation continues to the present. In the U.S the government's Bureau of Indian Affairs has continued to disregard promises and to be agents in the cheating of native people out of land, resources and revenues. The dishonesty of white traders to Indians is legend, and Native people understand that non-Indian dealers are not to be trusted.

What is not understood by either indigenous people or people of the dominant culture is that it is that culture which creates dishonesty in its constituents. Dishonesty is not a human characterisic. Human beings are naturally honest. Every baby tells the exact truth as far as she knows it. The concept of lying and dissembling must be taught to them. It is taught, of couurse, by fear. When a child becomes afraid of the repercussions of the truth, of the reactions of others, she learns to lie, in an attempt to protect herself,

Things to think about: Think about a lie someone has told you – or a lie that you have told. When someone lies to you, that person is afraid. Fear is the only reason that we lie. In a culture where everyone feels equally respected and cared about by everyone else, there is no motive for lying. Where people feel valued and safe and beloved within their society, there is no fear of others and no reason for dishonesty.

Native people, like simple country people the world over, honor a person who is as good as her word. We live by agreements with others, and cannot trust those agreements if we cannot trust their word. When a person is known to be as good as his word, there is no need for contracts and lawyers and affidavits.

All his life my friend Slow Turtle was known to one and all as a man of integrity and sometimes gritty honesty. He was also a man of great courage, which was the reason he could remain so honest in a mendacious and treacherous society. This courage was engendered by the support he received as a child by his family and his Indian community in Mashpee. He recalled that as a child he would listen to his father and his uncles talking around the kitchen table, getting much of his understanding of the world that way. One phrase his father often used stuck with him. The elder Peters would declare that "my word is as good as my bond," or that another's word was "as good as his bond."

One day in school, when Slow Turtle was about nine years old, a new principal assembled the student body to stand and recite the pledge of allegiance to the American flag. He noticed that young Slow Turtle did not stand. The principal asked him why he didn't want to make the pledge.

"I did that before already," Slow Turtle replied, "and my word is as good as my bond."

As we look at the world around us today we see few examples of honesty. I have before me now a book whose title is <u>You Are Being Lied To</u>, a giant, thick book that exposes media distortion, historical whitewashes and cultural myths. We have come to expect no truth from politicians, advertisers, business leaders or bankers. But I never met a native elder from any indigenous culture whose word I would not accept on anything.

WE CAN GET THROUGH THIS

We can get through this, you know,
If we stay together. It does
Get dark at times, there are noises
And silences we cannot fathom,
So we have only to stay very close,
Touch each other alive at dawn,
Learn each other well in the sunlight,
Hold together warm in stormy nights,
Sing our dreams to the starry ocean,
And whisper our truth in our ears.
I'll find reason and hope enough for us
Find that and more in you and love itself
And we'll get through this cozily my dear.

PART THREE

DIRECTION SOUTH - Trusting the Heart

ELEMENT FIRE

Three instructions to mend the sacred hoop of the people, or

TO BUILD A SOCIETY OF LOVE AND HAPPINESS

7. HUMILITY

8. GENEROSITY: THE GIVE-AWAY

9. HOSPITALITY

PART THREE – SOUTH

Now for the direction of the south I thought I would take a bigger leap and leave North America to go south of the equator, mid-point of our earth. There are more Amerindians here in South America than anywhere, and over the years I have met and talked with many of them, from countries which have oppressed them cruelly: Argentina, Uruguay, Paraguay, Chile, Peru, Ecuador, Bolivia, Venezuela, and Brazil – where I have taken us now. Brazil is a land with a long and terrible history of genocide of its indigenous populations by Europeans. Throughout much of this country today there is less evidence of racism, more harmony among its very diverse mix of Indians, African, European and Asian populations than in most nations today, yet many descendents of Portuguese and other immigrant peoples control most of the wealth, and in the pursuit of wealth traditional primitive tribes are still being exterminated. The great rain forests that control climate, air quality, and contain unknown medicines, are being destroyed for grazing land, to grow soybeans to feed farm animals and for fuel. We must take note of them, for they are problems – destruction of the environment and of native peoples and cultures, of greed and domination by the rich and powerful, that confront all our world, that we must address and redress if we are to survive at all.

It is not to confront these problems that I take us now to Brazil, I wanted to come south of the Equator for a different perspective. The southern hemisphere has far less people than we in the north, and we tend to overlook and forget that part in thinking about our world. Here are different cultures, different languages, different plants and animals, different stars in the sky, different seasons, opposite to ours. I wanted to take us out of our isolation, expand ourselves on the planet a little. When we stay only with our own people and ways we are very limited and narrow, and fail to understand our position as members of a single family on a small planet hidden away in the boondocks of one spiraling community of billions of suns.

For instance, instead of the solstice entering summer, our solstice here now ushers in winter, and the nights are long. Whereas now in Sweden, for instance, land of my wife's people, it will not get dark at all tonight and people will play and sing and dance around a pole with a crosstree that is adorned with leaves and flowers. That thought nicely jumbles our normal perspectives and forces us to think in broader global terms beyond the limits of our little lives. For those of us familiar with the families of stars we observe from our hemisphere it is quite disconcerting to look up at night, before the dawn as we do now, and see not the

North Star but the Southern Cross. It is exciting too. Space Ship Earth seems to be taking us star trekking – "to boldly go where no one has gone before!"

But I wanted to visit this land mainly because of its people. I have been here before, some years ago, to attend a global Rainbow Gathering in the highlands of Bahia. There we met many Brazilians, as well as other South and North Americans and people from Europe, Africa, Asia, Australia and Pacifica, giving us a really global feeling. I loved making music every night with people blending many cultures, but especially the musicians of Brazil. When we visited Salvador, capital city of Bahia, there was music everywhere, people playing on the streets, and a feeling of the joy of living and great friendliness from everyone. It was wonderful to me to be in a land where people's skins are many shades of brown and their smiles all bright and their hearts all warm!

This seemed to me to be a good place to explore the instructions for our hearts. The people here are not wealthy, there is little that is modern and new, everything looks a little bit worn down, but comfortable, lived in, like the old clothes you hang on to because you can't afford new ones and anyway you love them. But there is not great poverty either, no terrible slums, as in Sao Paulo, for instance, or starvation, as in much of the world. I didn't see homeless people, drunk or drugged people, and I was told there is little crime in Bahia. Everywhere we went the people seemed content, they laughed a lot and were very friendly.

So I have wanted for some time to return and bask in those good feelings again – much like the feelings in some of our Indian communities to the north – but with more music! Perhaps it is not as ideal as the memory I have from my short stay of only one week, but I felt connected and close immediately to the people I met, and it is my belief that this is how we human beings really are when we are not pressured by the greed and consumerism, the isolation and unfriendliness, the fears and frustrations of a domination culture. Even in the city I felt the old tribal values existing, the values of equality and respect, of helpfulness and mutual support, of individual freedom, creativity and joy in life and each other. To me, Bahia was a land with heart!

Now the Earth has circled another quarter around the sun, and we have come to the summer equinox. I had thought to keep our circles in Turtle Island – North America. But my heart kept tugging at me to go further, to go as far south as I have yet traveled, down to this magical state of Bahia. It was a grand journey with my old friends Felipe, Diamond Dave, and George and his daughter Cedar Rose. We danced in the streets with the friendly and musical people of the colorful city of Salvador, rented a VW van and drove torturous, cratered roads into the mountains, to celebrate there with people from all over the world, and of course many Brazilians and indigenous people. Afterwards we drove north along the coast to a small fishing village to meet a musician we had heard of at the gathering. We were the only guests at a small motel on the top of a cliff looking over the sea, and so, though we had little money, we were treated like royalty. I think this is a good beach for our circle now, beside the powerful tides of the great Atlantic, making a connection to our earlier circles to the north. It is a place I cannot forget, too, because here Tashin, my younger son, swam out by himself to rescue me from the inexorable undertow that threatened to carry me away to Antarctica!

On that morning I had looked down to the beach to see Ellika, my wife, walking briskly back and forth from the beach to the water's edge. Later I learned she had discovered many tiny new-born turtles blindly striking out for the ocean, vulnerable to birds of prey above, so she undertook to bring them all to safety and a presumably long life at sea. So I tried out the sea myself, and was enjoying the large surf when my son Tashin swam out to me and said I was being taken by undertow, which I had not noticed. So, mainly to oblige him, I struck our for the shore, thinking I am strong and have no problem, until some minutes later I discovered I had made no progress at all. Hard as I swam I stayed only in one place, and when I stopped I was moved inexorably outward again. The waves were too high for Tashin to help, but he stayed by my side, encouraging me on, "Come on, Pop, faster, you can do it!" And so slowly I progressed, growing more and more tired, and eventually was able to put my feet on ground and make it in. Tashin, no doubt also tired, sat with his head in his hands and wept as I had not seen him weep since he was a baby. My wife and Felipe came and put their arms around him and he sobbed, "I thought I was going to lose my Pop!" It was one of those moments of my life I will never forget, and the first thing I think of when I think of that beautiful empty beach. It brought us closer than I had felt since he was a small boy, and I will always treasure that – so for me this is a beach with great heart in my memory.

I promised myself I would return some day and had not been able to make it yet, but now that you know my story of this beach, let's form our circle there. It's very peaceful here, because although it is the solstice, here it is winter. The weather is mild and warm, being close to the equator, but there are no tourists. Just us on this long expanse of sand. Even the turtles have all hatched and scurried down to the water.

The sun is setting below the cliff behind us and the stars are beginning to show as the sky darkens. I love to star-gaze here in the southern hemisphere where there are so many unfamiliar objects to observe – the Southern Cross, of course, and the two small irregular galaxies named for Magellan, the first northerner to see them, the light from which began its journey to us 160,000 years ago.

Now we have built a small fire from driftwood and the darkened sky thrusts thousands of blazing stars forth for us, including Alpha Centauri, closest neighbor star, whose light has only taken four years to reach us. So, with all those neighbors blazing away above while we wait for First Light of our own star, Grandfather Sun, let us begin to consider the teachings that are most important for our living together in families and villages and nations. The instructions for the heart that we will consider here are those, which should govern our relationships with each other, in families and in community, with strangers, friends and lovers. How we may live together in a good way. The ones I have selected for this direction are Humility, Generosity and Hospitality.

7. HUMILITY

One of the characteristics that all the elders who have influenced me had in common was humility. They did not speak about it at all, except to tell the old stories in which a very arrogant and egotistical character might come to grief because of his boasting. But the elders were all very modest and unassuming, generally quite quiet unless asked to speak, and always giving credit to others and not taking it for themselves.

This is one of the Original Instructions we would do well to consider and think about and speak of more openly and more often, since elders rarely speak of it directly. They are examples of it in all they do and say, if you are paying attention. And the folly of arrogance, the opposite of humility, is a main and recurring theme in many of our stories, be they about Rabbit or Coyote or Raven or Iktome or Lox or Nanabush or whoever, they are often thinking too much of themselves and living to regret it. Today I would like to think more about that arrogance and where it comes from. They say the wisest man in the ancient world was Socrates. Remember what he said? "All I know is that I know nothing."

The scariest people are the true believers, those who think they know it all. They never listen and never learn, only want others to conform to their own ignorance. Do you know people who you think are arrogant? What do you think has made them that way?

Arrogance is a chief sin of the dominant culture. It began as that culture began in certain parts of the world six to ten thousand years ago. In earlier times it seems that all human beings were following their instructions. They lived in circles and took care of each one equally in those circles. They lived in harmony with the world around them and did not hold themselves above it.

I am told that civilization began in certain great valleys in the Near East and the Far East. These were places between or beside great rivers where the lands were conducive to the planting of seeds in broad and vast areas that the rivers irrigated. And so agriculture was begun on a grand scale, which produced a surplus of food and that produced a population explosion. It all must have happened too quickly for those long-ago people in those valleys. They did not understand that the instructions for human beings were to live in circles of equals, small enough to know each other's hearts and to care for each other.

As there were more and more people born and crowding together in those valleys the small circles were lost and with them the Original Instructions began also to be lost. When people no longer knew their neighbors they began to be isolated from each other. They did not know each other's hearts and began not to care. They became more independent and more isolated from each other, and without those close human ties and that close human contact they began to lose a little of that humanity, that good human nature with which they were born. Essential to that humanity is a sense of connection to other human beings, to other animals and plant life, to the wind, the rain and the Earth, the sun, moon, stars and all Creation. It is in our spirit to feel those relationships, in which we are all connected, and in which we are all equal.

They were still born trusting and hopeful for safety and love and fun. But after their circles, their clans, and their family closeness were destroyed they were born into a society from which those human qualities were fast disappearing and which immediately began to force and frighten those qualities from every child.

Another change in human activity was occurring at the same time. Animals were being domesticated for exclusive human ownership and usage. The domestication of plants and animals had a profound impact on the spirituality as well as the psychology of those long-ago people.

Imagine, for a million and more years people had lived in small circles that were united with common beliefs and understanding. They believed they were children of an earth mother who cared for them, and they were relatives to all the rest of earth's children, the plants and the animals.

No one could conceive that they could own any part of the earth, their own mother, or own any of the other independent beings that the earth supported. And so they evolved healthy and nourishing relationships with all these relatives. They made ceremonies for the earth, for the plants and animals, and made give-aways for them, asked for and thanked them for their support. In this way they recognized the sacredness of all beings. The people were not superior to the earth, but dependent upon it and devoted to it as loving children. They did not feel superior to the other creatures, but part of a great web where all were equal.

What a profound change occurred when man began to believe he was superior to everything in Creation! Now people believed they could own land and the earth became, not a loving mother, but an object for possession, for contention and conflict and even the shedding of blood and the taking of life. They could then own the plants and animals and treat or mistreat them however they chose. They began to contend and struggle with one another over that ownership.

When they learned to tame and ride the horse they could suddenly move faster over the earth than they had ever done before. Even though for thousands of years no one could go faster than a horse, now the desire for ever greater speed was stirred, and in modern times the steam locomotive, the internal combustion automobile, the airplane and space rockets propel us faster and faster. And the faster we go the more we need to be in further places sooner, and the more stressed we become.

Getting people onto horses allowed them to cover more territory and enter lands that were getting more and more filled with people. It is a small step from becoming the master of a horse to becoming a master of other people. The horse allowed a larger culture of herding animals, and the men who herded became dominators, not only of animals, but of each other.

However it happened, the change in human society from cooperation to domination resulted in the loss of equality, not only among species, but also among people. In a society of domination, some are dominators and some are dominated. And in every society where this happened it was men who were the dominators, never women. Women, who were closer to the earth, the home, the food, the children, to the heart of life. In a warrior society physical force and strength, violence and death are more honored than caring and nurturing, softness, tenderness, love and life. That half of the population whose work was peace and harmony, nurturing and caring, became subservient to the half whose ideals were power and violence, acquisition and domination, not only of goods but of people. Civilization began to be built on the backs of slaves.

Gone was the sense of sacredness in the earth and all things, in all life. Gone was the understanding of the equality and the connectedness of all things. Gone was the acceptance of responsibility for the balance and harmony in human relationship. Suddenly other human beings are not relatives but adversaries. The change in consciousness from cooperation to domination is the greatest and most fatal change that has taken place in the history of life on this planet.

Civilization advanced with the growing population, which began to condense in towns and market places on trade routes, and these towns became cities. At first these centers were peaceful as the people continued to honor and celebrate the gods or spirits that bring good weather and good harvests. Not everyone was needed in the fields to produce the food, so some developed individual skills and trades, becoming builders, tool makers, merchants, doctors, priests, entertainers and so on, exclusively.

But as wealth began to accumulate because of all these activities, it was accumulated more by some than others. Because people were no longer your relatives, it was not required by custom and morality for you to care for others or to share with others, even if you have much more than you need and others are starving. People no long saw themselves as equals in a single family. They saw each other as competitors. It was no longer embarrassing to have more than others On the contrary, it was thought of as proof of your superiority, and the rich became more honored than the poor.

So of course when domination and competition became the ideals and models for society the result was increasing conflict. Society became out of balance in its very structure. In such a society there can never be peace and harmony, by its very nature.

Eventually the struggle for control is bound to become violent. Human nature is inherently cooperative and peaceful and caring and fun-loving. But when human children are delivered into societies of inequality, of competition and conflict, when the adults that raise them are engaged in the struggle for domination, it is fear and not love that will guide their thoughts and actions with others.

Due to the breakdown of the circle, the community of equals that care for each other, the nomadic herding families came into conflict with each other more and more and developed a warrior way of life, exalting strength, bravery, competition, and aggression in the individual rather than kindness, humility, nurturing, and peacefulness.

From this way of life proceeded a hierarchy developed from the skills of violence and patriarchy. No longer were people equals as they had been for millions of years. Now the warrior and the chief were not the servants of the people but their masters. Women, children, the old and the infirm had no voice in this new society.

Similar changes were going on in the urban civilizations. Wealth, in this new system, is power. And without the closeness of the circle, without the common spiritual beliefs in respect and equality and humility, without honoring the elders who transmit these original instructions, this power of wealth corrupts. Those who learned how to amass wealth through whatever means of effort , skill, shrewdness and sheer force also learned how to protect that wealth, to hire others not only to protect but also to accumulate more wealth.

So hierarchies of power were created. Warlords became kings, kings became emperors. The structure and existence of such a society must be gained and held by violence. And so the king must have his palace guards and his army, he must send them to capture land and resources and people. People to pay his tribute and taxes, to conscript into his army, and to become the slaves to build his cities and temples. He will establish a nobility and pay off priests to support him. Rich merchants will pay for his protection and dungeons will be built for those who oppose him.

When the raiding nomadic tribes attacked wealthy cities they saw how easy it was for a violent people to subdue a peaceful people. So soon after attacking they stayed and changed the way of those people from cooperation and veneration of life and the spirit, to a way of fear and conflict and domination.

When kingdoms expanded and became empires and overran other societies the culture of violence grew and extended itself. These warring nations naturally concentrated their attention and knowledge on the arts of violence and the creation of ever greater weapons. And so the whole history of this civilization in which we struggle today is a history of violence and the spreading of this violent way of life inevitably across the globe. In the Americas are many of the most recent victims of this conquest, including the first nations of my land.

There are not so many kings and emperors any more, some few dictators and warlords as in olden times. People decry that 'tribalism', but that is corrupted modern tribalism, far from our tribes of old where all were equal." But the lords of today are the CEOs, the boards of directors and managers of the business world. The empires of today are multi-national corporations, and world conquest is now called globalization.

The situation, philosophically, psychologically, economically, and spiritually, is the same as under the pharaohs, the khans, the Caesars or the czars. The earth, our mother, is still an object to be bought and sold and conquered by arrogant human creatures. Human beings are still being taught by this society of violence that domination of our relatives the plant and animal people is a good and natural thing. The domination of human beings over each other is not even questioned. The use of violence by one state against another is not questioned. Poverty, racism, oppression are generally unquestioned. The fact that six percent of the people in the world own most of the earth and its resources is not questioned. That's how it is. That's the system.

People will tell you with a straight face, with great earnestness, that it's the best system ever devised. If you do question it they will say you're a radical, unpatriotic, dangerous, why don't you go somewhere else? What are you a communist, an anarchist, a troublemaker, a terrorist? That's how they keep the status quo. And that's pure ignorance. Because of course it is not the best system ever devised. We have done better. Much better.

For millions of years we had no war, no kings, no armies, no police, no criminals, no prisons, no sexism, no racism, no adultism, no oppression, no domination of other people or other species. We were not arrogant. We didn't think we were the only important creatures in the Creation.

When you lose that humility, when you think it's all right for human beings to lord it over everything in Creation, to own the earth and the other creatures, then you open the door to people lording it over each other. From believing human beings to be the only important species it's a natural step to believing you are the only human being of importance – your family having importance by their connection to you. It's an easy step to believing only your nation is important, only your race, only your sex, only your age or class or whatever.

It is unbelievably arrogant for a species to deface a mountain by carving the features of national leaders upon it. But it is more incredibly arrogant for a people to say that they have the best of all nations because by conquering and oppressing and stealing outright from other nations they have made themselves rich at the expense of most of the world's people who live in poverty.

It is not just arrogant, it is plain foolish to believe that people are happier because of the accumulation of wealth. Of course all human beings are entitled to basic human needs, to have adequate shelter, fuel, food and medical care. But beyond that it is not material wealth that brings happiness. Quite the contrary. What makes us happy are our close and loving connections to people and to the natural world, and the free exercise of our creativity. In general the accumulation of material things gets in the way of that.

It is arrogant of us to think that the invention and acquisition of new gadgets, new toys better than the old toys, are going to take the place of love and caring, of touching and of serving Creation. But that arrogance is born of alienation and loneliness and the lack of love and caring, touching, and serving, in the world we inhabit.

True humility would suggest to us that if this world is so badly out of balance and bids fair to destroy its own home on earth, there is something very wrong with the way we are living our lives. Humility would direct us to seek solutions beyond those of the society that has initiated and continued this destruction.

In humility we should listen to our children and young people to whom we bequeath this confused unhappy world. They are closer to the spirits in nature and to the sources of joy. They see clearly what society is manifesting and are appalled by the immorality, the selfishness, and the arrogance of the world they face. Only they have not a clear idea how they may effect the right changes in the system. How to proceed from the mess we have handed them to the world of their dreams. Meanwhile society marginalizes them as "dreamers", "idealists", and impractical. What is more impractical than the world this society has fashioned for us?

In humility we should listen to the elders and the visionaries. The elders who carry the remembrances of when people lived in balance, cooperating and sharing. The visionaries who can dream the way back to the path of balance and harmony.

Things to think about: Do you think other people see you as having humility? There are two important things to understand about people who display honest humility. First is that they are self-confident but don't think about themselves a lot. Second is that they do think about other people and that with a measure of tolerance. It's like they are thinking, "Look, nobody's perfect, we're all flawed, but we do the best we can and we need to support each other." So. How's your confidence, and how's your compassion?

Humility will tell us to be grateful to a power beyond ourselves for the intelligence as well as the life we have been given and not to squander them on the superficial distractions we have fashioned, but to put them in the service of this glorious Creation.

THEOLOGY 101

Really, don't you think we must drop
All this stuff about God? Dump it?
Delete it. It's blinding us really.
We get too arrogant or too complacent
With our constructs. Kick the props out
And we might cling to honest humility.
That's all that allows the possibility
In the vastness of our ignorance to perceive
Any new thing which may stretch
A further reach to what might really be.

8. GENEROSITY: THE GIVE-AWAY

When people follow the Original Instructions to live in a circle, as equal beings who respect each other, who care for every member of the circle, who work together cooperatively for the common good and share with each other what they need for survival, it is not possible for anyone to be too poor. But it is possible, due to their differences in energy, skills, and interests, for some people to accumulate more material possession than others. Far more than they need.

Now in a society whose values are centered on sharing and caring for each other, and on equality, excessive wealth is viewed as an embarrassment. An encumbrance. A sign that perhaps that person's values are shifting. He is becoming unbalanced, thinking more about material things than of his people. Eventually such misplaced attention will lead to alienation, selfishness, and greed.

So it was for many people in former times, that when a person found himself with an embarrassing accumulation of possessions, he would decide to give away most of them, whatever was not essential to his survival. He might make a present to certain persons in need, or he might announce a formal social event - a "give-away". This might often be part of a feast to which all were invited, such as for instance the potlatch of the northwest, or it might be part of other spiritual ceremonies, as my people are accustomed to do. Or the person might spread his possessions before his lodge and invite everyone to choose something - kind of a free yard sale.

These give-aways were often motivated by an exceptional occurrence in the person's life - a marriage, the birth of a child or grandchild, a name-giving, a new work or other achievement by a family member, the recovery of a family member from illness or a return home by one long away. Grief might also occasion such an event, especially over a death in the family.

The truth of the old adage "it is better to give than to receive" is born out again and again. When we get a present from someone we often have mixed feelings about it. It is hard just to accept it in the spirit in which it is given if we aren't absolutely sure of that spirit. We may wonder about the motivations of the giver. We may wonder if he can truly afford to give such a gift. We stammer out silly things like "you really shouldn't have". We may even feel a bit embarrassed or unworthy.

It is different when we are the giver. There is no question of our own motivations in giving. We give out of love. We give out of gratitude to the Creation and to those we are gifting. We learn that this is an unmitigated pleasure always available to us. The more we give the better we feel, the happier we become. And the less stuff we have to organize and fuss over preserving and keeping safe.

In the more ritualized setting of a Give-Away there should be no question about the motives of the giver. He wishes to honor you. He acknowledges your kinship to him. In receiving, you acknowledge that honoring and that kinship.

We may also notice that by restricting our possessions to a few simple needs we are also happier. Life is simpler, less complicated, without a lot of things to take care of, things that can actually take over our lives as they demand our attention. It is a dependable measure of your distance from happiness - the number of things you call "mine". Jesus told his listeners to sell all they had and give it to the poor. The Buddhist Dhammapada says "Sorrow cannot touch the man who is not in the bondage of anything, who owns nothing." I try to tell myself that the few things I keep in my house, mainly books and music, are only the bare necessities for my mind and soul - then I continually lose things in the mess, and I think how peaceful yet full my life might be if I lived in an even smaller wetu with only sufficient garments and tools and my sacred bundle.

I remember a Russian story about a man who bet his friend a fortune that he could not stay voluntarily in a solitary cell for ten years. The prisoner was allowed books and read all the time, eventually devouring all the spiritual wisdom ever written in every tradition. Meanwhile the man had a reversal and lost all his fortune. He was desperate, thinking perhaps he would have to kill his friend if he won. But ten minutes before the end of ten years the prisoner left his cell. He had proven his point, but he had also become enlightened and realized that in winning a fortune he would lose that happiness. So he renounced all worldly treasure.

Sometimes I relate this tale to the prisoners, and they can understand it very well. If you offered them a million dollars to stay a year longer than their sentences they would refuse, because freedom is without price. They understand the instructions of the Give-Away naturally and are always thinking of what they can give to their families and their children. They are so grateful for the gift of the circle, which has given them their lives again, that they often speak of how they wish to give back. To bring the circle into prisons that have none. To bring the circle into schools, into boys' clubs, into the streets, into gangs. To share the great gift they have received. To help others find the good red road and stay off the path of destruction that brought them down.

Because the spiritual instruction that urges the Give-Away is not limited to giving material things. A pure love is a great Give-Away. A pure love wants nothing for itself, wants only that the beloved be fulfilled in every way, be healthy, be happy, be at peace with himself. This love says to the beloved, "I see you. I recognize you. I know who you are. You are one of Creation's radiant and glorious creatures. You are unique, and your gift is needed by this world. I will always be there to remind you of your true self when you forget, get confused or discouraged. I am happy you exist, and your being honors me with its presence."

Likewise your smile can be a powerful gift. With it you may silently and immediately convey pure love to another. Whomever you smile upon, dear friend or stranger, you will raise her spirits, give her confidence in herself, the encouragement of your support and good will, the warmth of human closeness, and the possibility that after all life may be good. All that can happen on a subconscious level from a simple exercise of face muscles coupled with the light of good will and love that burns within.

Because of course if we are not feeling that love and that joy in others our smiles will be forced and false. Then again, many people are so sad and desperate and needy they do not notice. They grab whatever straw of support that seems to be offered and are grateful. Also there is the phenomenon that when you do uplift those muscles in your face you may also begin to affect your own mood. A smile can remind us of our positive effect and worth in the world as we see its effect on others. If it reminds us of our relationship to the one we smile on, it may remind us of our deep relationship to others and to all beings, and bring us once more to recollection and gratitude to Creation.

So perhaps it is better to smile. If we use that Give-Away as an instruction, as a discipline, we will develop it more and more by practise and spend more and more time in the state of awareness of our blessings instead of attention to our distresses.

The elders often told us that we were unique. You have been given a special gift by the Creator, they would say. No one in the long story of the world ever had a gift exactly like it, and no one ever will again. If you don't know what that gift is, you better look for it. Because if you don't find it and develop it and give it away, it will be lost to the world forever. Your purpose, the reason Creation gave you this life, is to use that gift. And in using it, to give it away. To give it back to Creation.

All the great thinkers, the wise ones, the writers, artists, musicians, scientists, discovered their gifts and developed them and gave them back to the world. And the world is richer for that. But greatness has not to do with breadth or fame. Your gift may be as a parent, a teacher, a gardener, a fisherman, a tailor, a cook, a storyteller, a friend, a healer, a singer, a tinker, a technician, or a dreamer. It may be that you notice need and are drawn to create a response to it.

It seems there is a great spiritual need in the world today. The twentieth century in its vicious, immoral, heartless acts of violence, war, oppression and greed has confused and hardened the hearts of those who survived them. I was born in the nineteen twenties, at the height of optimism in industrialized America, before Wall Street laid an egg, as the <u>Variety</u> headlines put it. The dream came crashing down. The war to end all wars had been fought, but then the Japanese invaded Manchuria, the Italians invaded Ethiopia, and the Germans marched into the Sudetenland.

We still thought we could fix it all. We human beings. Make it all come right. We struggled out of the great depression, defeated the enemies of freedom, and settled down to live in peace and prosperity forever.

The God that promoted violence and greed, that God was dead, we thought. The God that sent our races and religions to war with each other in His name, that told us to kill and torture each other for blasphemy and heresy, that plundered the peoples of far lands, commiting genocide for His glory, and lining the coffers of the kings and the priests, that God, it seemed, was dead. Copernicus and Galileo and Darwin and Freud had put man and his gods in their places. Human beings were not the center of Creation and the masters of the universe. They were not special to the Divinity who reserved a future for them in a Paradise or Samadhi or Nirvana. Human beings were pathetic little braggards who were desperately trying to distract themselves and forget the horror of their own annihilation

As one of the favorite slogans of business people at the close of that century put it: "the one who dies with the most toys wins!"

A large percentage of the world population had been convinced by science that God was a construct of earlier ignorant peoples' wish-fulfillment fantasies. Existence could ultimately be comprehended without recourse to the notion of an all-encompassing intelligence. It was not designed, it just happened. And we get to spend three, four, perhaps five score years in this accident, trying to make the best we can out of that. So too, people accepted that this notion of a soul, which no one can locate or measure, may also be discarded. It is a disorienting situation, to say the least, after all these centuries of reliance on revealed truth from sacred scritpture.

The relatively small number of reactionaries known as fundamentalists rightly enjoin against the immorality of contemporary culture, but take up a rear-guard action loudly and fiercely in stances they proclaim to be moral but are clearly immoral, condoning violence, advocating separatism, coercion, sexism, authoritarianism.

The rest of the world pretty much agrees that the pursuit of happiness here on earth is what the years of our lives should be about. Strangely this essential ingredient is not taught in our educational systems, not discussed until college philosophy classes, nor by panels of sages or philosophers in public forums, and is not even deeply thought about or probed by the average person picking his way through the complexities of the modern world.

The education supplied by the culture as a whole asserts that human happiness may be derived from material wealth. Although, as we have seen, this is contrary to the teachings of all the sages and spiritual traditions and to the folk wisdom of rural people everywhere, mainstream culture asserts it nevertheless. From childhood to retirement the public is seduced into consumerism with the assertion that all they need to be happy is this particular item that is to be on sale all week. You can be sexier. Have more fun, be more popular, more beautiful, be more relaxed, healthier, younger, remove drudgery, boredom, be smart, up to date, be cherished - even better be envied - if you buy this, buy that, buy, buy, buy. The only important part of education, we learn, is training to get well-paid jobs or start successful businesses.

So the only measure of your success as a human being is always how much are you worth? And the success of any enterprise, in publishing, in theatre, and film, in art and music, in medicine and healing, in journalism and education, invention, discovery - is only measured by its profitability. Which is why this culture is simply bereft of imagination, creativity, or spirituality. It is boring, formulaic, pedestrian, superficial, desperately striving for novelty and tittilation and excitement.

Small wonder everyone feels limited, confined to a "rat race", restless, overworked, overscheduled, overstressed, with no end in sight this side of retirement or the grave. I want to ask people if they believe that as they look back on their death-beds they think they will feel sorry they did not put in more overtime, invest better, make more money to leave behind. What will they think it was all about, all those years of stress and confusion? And that new house, the home theatre, the Lexus and the BMW, the annual vacation in Hawaii, did that make it worth while? Will they feel at peace, in love, their purpose on earth fulfilled? Or will the hours and years of their lives appear a meaningless waste? Or will they feel or think at all?

And of course there are many people who are concerned with the lack of satisfaction, the emptiness, the restless striving of contemporary life. Millions of people, feeling that void, sensing or hoping there must be more to existence, are actively searching for answers. They read the latest book on the latest approach to spirituality, the latest therapy, the latest aid to meditation. They go to classes in yoga, tai chi, Sufi dancing, feng shui.

They attend seminars or watch the self-help gurus on TV. Having long abandoned the religion of their parents, they convert to another, perhaps leap-frog through many over the years. They are attracted, ever hopeful, to shamans everywhere. In the Amazon, among aboriginal dreamers or Hawaiian kahunas. They try peyote, sacred mushrooms, ayahuasca. They fast and meditate and go on vision quests. They have statues of St. Francis or Buddha or Siva-Sakti, framed pictures of Ramakrishna or the Dalai Lama or Meher Baba.

Still, most are unsatisfied. Something is missing. They believe there is more, but they have no idea where to find it or even how to search. For instance, the fellow they called Joe the Plumber, who confronted candidate Barack Obama in the 2008 election because he was concerned about being taxed too much after he had reached an income of $250,000! Imagine that! Most of the world is struggling to get food and shelter and this man is worried he won't have enough after he earns a quarter million! And people take that seriously! Shameless – They are not even embarrassed to whine for more than their fair share when so many are starving and homeless. That comes from a lack of community, resulting in a lack of humanity. They should be thinking about having a give-away! Americans would be shocked to learn how much the Scandinavian peoples pay in income taxes – but they are rated the happiest countries on Earth, the ones with the most desirable standard of living for every person. There is no great wealth and no poverty. Everyone has a full education, complete and excellent medical care, plenty of vacation time and retirement income, and they preserve and care deeply for their beautiful natural environment. It is unfortunate that fear engendered by the influx of asylum seekers from other lands creates in some there a new selfishness that wants to undo the great achievements of that society.

At this point I would suggest that a good starting point might be to look at and contemplate the lives of people who appear to be balanced, centered, at peace, who know who they are, whose lives have purpose and meaning. Who, for instance? Well, you wouldn't know my elders who have left us, but some names might come to mind, because we know some of the more famous ones. We are attracted and fascinated by their lives. Names from the last century, like Albert Schweitzer, Helen Keller, Mahatma Gandhi, Dag Hammarskjold, Martin Luther King Jr, Mother Teresa, and some still living their examples: the Dalai Lama, Nelson Mandela, Desmond Tutu, Thich Nhat Hahn.

What do these people have in common? They each saw a need and were called by their natures, their understanding of their particular gifts, by their souls if you like, to address those needs and to persist, through hardship and sacrifice, to address that need with all of their gifts for all of their lives.

Service. To serve Creation with all our gifts through all the days of our lives. That is the great Give-Away. There is no truer font of happiness than that. Of course, most of those people would not speak of their happiness. They are too busy, too engaged, their attention and energy directed out, to be giving any attention to their own happiness. An irony perhaps, but not a paradox.

And in those moments of pause, taken for the self, for the soul, no doubt they have drunken the sun, the stars, the rain of spring, the heat of summer, the freshness of fall, the quiet of winter, and they have smiled. Knowing all is well. It is good. It is right.

I could take you with me now to visit other happy people I have met. Not famous people with legendary lives. Simple, ordinary people. Not wealthy.

Industrial society would locate them far below the poverty line. But with a home that can be kept warm and dry and with enough to eat. They can be found in far places all over the world. Those I know best live in North America, mostly far from urban centers, with a still unbroken connection to the land and to a community.

The ones I know, you wouldn't call their lives easy. Life for them is an ongoing struggle. Not just a lack of luxury and conveniences. Real tragedy haunts every family as members have been torn from them by the cruel but seductive culture that has infested their ancient lands and ways. Alcoholism and its deadly accidents and the despair that weighs upon the young, missing relatives pulled from the community and lost, perhaps to prison.

And yet, the ones I speak of, they do more than merely survive this onslaught of the dominant white culture. They are strong. With tragedy continually threatening they do not despair. They are humorous and joke affectionately with one another. They love their children and their old ones. They do not complain of themselves. When something is to be done, they do it. When nothing can be done, they find something else to do.

Would you say they are happy? If you asked them they would make a joke about it. But come and visit with me and see for yourself. We are greeted at the door and invited to come in. Their pleasure in our visit is evident and genuine. Hospitality in this house is not formal, it is relaxed and natural, warm and nourishing as the food we are quickly served. They show a friendly interest in our lives and concerns. The children run and play freely about us, sometimes listening, sometimes asking us questions, laughing a lot. There is an atmosphere here pervading this home that each one knows but will not name. It is strong enough, however, to spill over on all who come through their door. Perhaps we should call it love.

So what is the ingredient here - the one we are looking for that links this happiness to that of the famous people we were just speaking of? Is there a common instruction underlying what we can perceive as true happiness in the world? Or fulfillment, if you prefer that word? I think there is. Perhaps several.

For one thing, respect. That was evident as we came through the door. These people respected us and themselves, clearly. And humility. There was no pretension, no trying to seem better, no guile or manipulation. But I think there is more, though it may not seem as evident as in the case of our famous people. There is a sense of service. Probably the humility is a requirement for that, as well as respect.

What is this sense of service? The sense of responsibility for ones own home, for ones spouse and children, are still felt universally around the world. But tribal peoples and for many other poor and simple folk of rural traditions everywhere there is still a much stronger connection to and feelings of responsibility for parents, brothers and sisters, nieces and nephews, aunts and uncles, grandparents - the whole spectrum of relatives of an extended family. There is an ingrained love of the land, not just one's proprietary holdings, but for the sacred sites and the places inhabited by ancestors, and that feeling extends to all the earth and all the fellow creatures that share it.

This sense of responsibility manifests as service, to Creation, the environment, to all of nature, to one's family and clan, to one's people. It engenders a lifelong role as protector and caretaker. The universal and striking phenomenon of hospitality and generosity to strangers probably began in the same feeling of responsibility, extending it beyond one's own people to all of humanity.

This is the sense of service which lay behind the devotion of those famous ones we spoke of before. A feeling of responsibility for others beyond one's own family and tribe. The sick of Africa's interior for Livingston and Schweitzer, the subjugated Indian people of all religions for Gandhi, the poorest of the poor of Calcutta for Mother Teresa. Dag Hammarskjold's life was dedicated and sacrificed in the service of peace for all people of earth.

The people I am speaking of here, the famous and the obscure, all felt themselves to be caretakers. What they did and do day by day - their motivations are not material wealth, fame, prestige or renown for themselves. Humble people all, their work, their dedication is service. These people usually think of themselves as servants. Some would say they serve God, or Creation, or humanity, or love, or hope. Whatever it is, they are serving something more than themselves, more than their families. They may not have a clear concept of what it is they serve, but it is outside and beyond themselves.

But it is also inside ourselves, as the Creator spirit resides in each of us. In those Original Instructions. These were the instructions heard by Schweitzer, Mother Teresa and the rest of them when the need was shown to them. These are the instructions that have kept First Nation people dedicated to the land, to family and community, and helped them survive one of the greatest holocausts of human history, the taking of their lands and livelihood and millions and millions of innocent lives. But not only have the people survived, albeit still in the state of oppression, racism, poverty and unredeemed tragedy, but they have survived with heart and with spirit, with a sense of humor, generosity, kindness, and a dedication to life, to the earth, to the future, to all Creation.

Like many ancient peoples, the North American natives have a strong sense of love and connection, gratitude and responsibility to their ancestors. But they are more unusual in their sense of responsibility and commitment to the unborn, to the future generations of whom we are the ancestors. When that is a firm and understood dedication, the attitudes about actions in the present are profoundly affected.

At bottom our people's attitude is this: we are unbelievably fortunate. To have been given this immense and immeasurable gift of life. And not just the life of a microbe or an amoeba, or a bit of leaf-mold or a snail, but to be walking, thinking, feeling human beings who are conscious of our connectedness to a vast universe beyond us. We have the idea, the feeling (the Instruction?) that it is not right to accept all this as our due and squander it in whatever way we choose. Even that ability to choose is a great gift.

Our first choice, then, the choice that seems necessary and right, our first act must always be to give thanks. We wake and give thanks for another dawn. Before we begin our work we acknowledge and give thanks to all our relatives and to the Creator, the Great Source of all. But the thought, the words are not enough. Action is needed. Work is prayer in action. Every act, every step we take, the elders say, should be our prayer. Action that is prayer is action that is in service to the Great Mystery, the Giver of our existence. To that Giver we return our thanks as service - our Give-Away.

Things to think about: Do you ever give a gift to someone when it's not a birthday or holiday? Is there someone you could surprise in that way with a thoughtful gift that shows you know the private wishes of the person? How about a lawn sale where the things are not for sale but free? What about cleaning out your house, all the stuff that clutters your life, the books you have read and won't read again, and just have a give-away? Invite your friends for a pot-luck and give-away party? Does your recycling center have a free table?

Can you imagine living in the kind of world where having more than other people would be shameful and embarrassing? Can you imagine an economy not based on wealth, nor even on trade, but on giving?

When you make a gift to someone you love, you want to make it the very best. So you need to know what it is you can do best. What you do best will come not only from the skill of your hands and your cleverness, it will come from your heart and soul. Before you can engage and integrate all that, you have to know who you are. Who you really are, not just your role in society, as a child of your parents, a member of your family, community and nation. That is one of the reasons why our people may sometimes separate themselves from society for a while, to sit by themselves alone in the natural world to find their reality, who they are apart from the roles they are given in society. Not who other people have said they are, or want them to be, but who Creation says they are.

"Creation loves you." These are the words of a song we sing in the sweat lodge. Creation loves you and wants you to be yourself, your true self as you were delivered into this existence. You are Creation's beloved child. Creation wants you to be the most of who you truly are, to know your true nature and to know your gifts. When you understand what your most special gift is, you need to learn all about it, to develop it, to use it. And then to give it away. To give back to Creation your developed gift from the truth of your being.

The elders I have known were the soul of generosity. They gave unceasingly of themselves, of their time and attention, of their caring and support, and, though they were poor materially, always shared whatever little they had.

GIVING

Giving is part of what we are here for.
Our lives are our greatest gifts, right? And you,
You are Creation's gift to the world. Oh, yes.
In all your variety and uniqueness, a great gift.

Never was anyone like you, in all the history
Of the world, and never will be one again
Just like you. So. You are it. The only one.
The gift you were given is like no other.

And what will you do with it? This precious life.
The only treasure there is. Will you keep it
Hidden away? What are you here for anyway?
That song, your own life, your special way

Of seeing and feeling and understanding,
That gift you alone were given is meant
To be given away. That's how I see it.
We've all got this great gift, life, our self,

And we're supposed to give it away to the world.
To share our selves with each other, to increase
Each other and add to the wonder. I mean,
What do you think you're looking for out there?

Oh, I see you, running, running, no time, not
Stopping, trying to catch up to something.
What is it? What do you miss? You seem full
Of distractions, small things, but also, it seems,

A yearning, a longing, something you want,
You search for. Do you know what it is?
Maybe it's me. Not just me, of course, but
All of us. We are waiting.. We lost each other.

(Now we keep to ourselves. If we reach out and
Get disappointed, we pull back again. Not safe.)
That's not true: we didn't get too close, we didn't
Get close enough. Deeper, deeper yet, we all

Every single one alive on Earth, we are longing
For each other. We need each other. It's family.
And only dysfunctional because we've been hurt,
And we are afraid. That's all it is. Really.

So what it takes is courage. The courage to give.
No expectation, no trade, just a free gift, yourself.
Part of yourself anyway. To start. Who knows
How far it goes? When I am with you now

I want to stop thinking "please". In my longing
I want to offer myself: "Here I am. I'm yours."
What part of me can you use? It's only to say
"Thank you." Thank you for being in my life.

My life is richer, wider, taller, with you in it.
Yes, it's true, Giving is what we are here for, and
We can just choose, we can really choose
To have each other completely, now and forever.

9. HOSPITALITY

There is a story about a raggedy, dirty, scruffy looking traveler who came weary to the lodge of a family. The turtle shell hanging by the door showed that this family was of the Turtle Clan. He asked the woman who came to the door if he might come in and rest for a bit, as he was tired.

"Who are you? Where are you from?" the woman asked. He told her she would not know his people, that he was from very far away. She looked at him the way some people look at hoboes, or gypsies, or hippies.

"I'm sorry, I don't know you. You must go somewhere else."

The wanderer went on until he came to a lodge whose antlers above the door showed this family was Deer Clan. Again he asked if he might come in and rest. Once more he was rejected. They said they did not know him.

At last he came to another lodge, and this one had bear claws above the door. The woman there took only one look, and before he could speak she took his arm.

"Look at you!" she said, "You are all dirty and dusty and you smell quite bad, your clothes are torn and your hair is a terrible mess!" And she took him inside and right away brought food for him and water to clean himself.

"You are tired, you must stay here for the night," she said, and while he slept she brought him new clothes and moccasins for his journey. But in the morning he was unable to rise, being sick with a raging fever. He described to her some herbs she could find nearby. When she administered these as he told her, the sickness quickly disappeared. But now it was too late to travel, so she fed him again, and once more he slept.

In the morning a different sickness was upon him, with many sores all over his body. He again described to her the herbs that could cure him. The woman spent a long time searching until she found the right plants. She put an infusion of these on the sores and they disappeared.

Once again he woke in the morning with a new disease, told her how to find and prepare the proper medication to heal him. This same story was repeated for many days. Then one morning the man rose strong and well.

"Now you know how to heal your people of many diseases. This is my give-away for your hospitality." He left and went on his way, and since that time it has been the way of those people that the knowledge of herbs and doctoring was passed down from generation to generation in the Bear Clan.

This story, and many, many others like it, shows how important the instruction of hospitality has been to our people. It also shows that there is an instruction for the recipient of that hospitality to acknowledge it in some way.

The Pawnee-Otoe-Missourian writer Anna Lee Walters relates that when her uncle came to visit he always brought something to eat. The Pawnee custom, she wrote, was that the warrior should bring food, preferably meat.

The instruction of hospitality is ingrained in people all over the world. Even today you may be traveling in some far land among people who do not know you and experience this hospitality. Especially among simple poor folk far from the centers of the "civilized" world, and always among indigenous people living still their traditional customs.

When you come to the door of such a family you will be greeted warmly, with great smiles of happiness to see you. You feel at once the sincerity of this, that they are truly glad you have come so that they may know you and you may learn of them.

The very first thing they will do is to have you sit while they bring something to eat and drink. This is primary, that the traveler rest and be given nourishment. No matter if that family has only a little food they will give it, and if they have not enough will send someone to borrow from a neighbor, who of course understands the demand of hospitality.

They will bring forth their greatest joys, their children and grandchildren, who will be very curious about you. Other children will probably learn of your visit and crowd into the room to see you, and they may ask many questions, about your own children and where and how you live.

They will ask you to stay longer than you had planned, and when you leave they will wish to give you a gift. Usually that will be something of themselves, something one of them has made that contains an expression of beauty from their own heart. I have many such things from my travels, and whenever I look at them I remember the good people who insisted I have it and take a little bit of their spirit, a little of their dreams with me.

Now contrast this, if you will, with an imaginary visit to someone in a big city apartment. There are no clans there, no village or community life. They don't even <u>know</u> their neighbors. They are afraid, terrified of strangers, and even of each other. There are triple or quadruple locks on their doors, a peephole, and a chain. If they don't know you they won't want to know you, like the people in the first two lodges of the Bear Clan story. And it gets worse the richer the neighborhood. The next more expensive building will be locked from outside, with buttons to push and speakers so the inhabitants can ask who you are before they buzz you in. Richer yet they also have security guards inside. In the suburbs we find signs: "No trespassing," "Keep out," "Beware the dog." The really fancy neighborhoods may be walled fortresses with a guarded gate. The richest being kingdoms to themselves, television cameras observe the portals and the grounds, notices that alarm systems are in operation, and the local police prowling often in their cars.

Yes, I have visited those places. They don't say "come in, you need to rest, have something to eat," even though they have so much. They only ask who are you and what do you want.

Now of those pictures of how people are living their lives at this very moment in our world, which ones seem to you the happiest, and which seem the most miserable? Their culture tells them that the richest ones should be the happiest. But they are clearly the fearful, the suspicious, the worried, the anxious, the closed-minded with the closed-homes. I would feel despair if I had to live with such wealth. Since I left the cities behind almost forty years ago there has never been a lock on my door. I have nothing anyone would want to steal, only blankets and baskets and pottery and beaded and carved things made by other open-hearted people I have visited.

But if you come to our house, my wife or I will start the kettle boiling and begin to pull things from the cupboards to feed you right away. We'll make up a bed for you if you can stay the night, even though we have no guest room in our tiny hand-made house in the woods, and you must sleep in the living room (the kitchen and my office are too small).

Writing about the Dakota <u>hunka</u> ceremony, Ella Cara Deloria quoted the official who performed it, in presenting his credentials, "I have gladly accepted the obligation of hospitality. No one in need has opened my tipi entrance in vain."

When I am asked to officiate a marriage ceremony, I address the families of the bride and groom and all of the gathered community with this reminder of our old ways and instructions. I tell them that this couple creating a new family unity is also part of the families of both sides and the family of the whole community. The children they will have will be the children of all of us. Our doors must be open to them at all times. If they have hard times, if they need food or shelter or medicine or just the warmth and love of their people, we must not wait for them to suffer bravely in silence. We must come forward and take them into the caring bosom of our own family.

The Original Instructions tell us to live in harmony within this Creation of which we are all a part. To stay in harmony we are instructed to respect all Creation, every being that exists, and to live as relatives to all. To maintain harmony all must be treated equally and feel they are equal to all. So we are instructed to live in a circle. This will keep the harmony in our community, in our village, in our clan, our lodge. For this harmony to be universal we must also be in accord with those who are distant, those of other communities and nations with perhaps cultures and ways that are strange to us. And so we have this very important instruction of hospitality, so that wherever we go we may be well received and well treated, and anyone coming to our door will be able to rely on the same.

This was the instruction that, as far as I can determine, was observed all over Turtle Island before the fateful invasion from Europe. Since I have found it in many places beyond Turtle Island and have had people tell me they found it all over the world, in South America, Africa, Australia, many island nations, and even many places in Europe, I believe this instruction was once universally followed by all of our ancestors everywhere.

As we now understand, this instruction was driven from the culture of the invaders many thousands of years ago, so they have forgotten it. Because of the fear. The fear, the greed, and the violence they stirred up were imported with the conquerors to remain at the center of the dominant culture all over the world.

That greed took hold of people like a fever and convinced them they didn't need each other. That it was better to have many things just for yourself or your close family than to have the love and support of your big family. The greed was reinforced by the fear, that others would take what you have, and behind the fear was always the threat and the actuality of violence.

When the invaders began coming to Turtle Island our people did not know that they were people who had lost their instructions. They had no understanding that a whole culture could become crazy and sick with greed, fear, and violence. They didn't realize the strange looking foreigners considered our people to be inferior beings, less than human. They would not have imagined that many of these boat people would think nothing of lying, cheating, stealing, even killing just to possess land and things they wanted

Naturally our people followed their instructions and opened their arms and their houses to the visitors. They fed them, helped them to plant their gardens, showed them the good places to fish and hunt and get drinking water, taught them skills of survival, smiled upon them and called them their white brothers. Some people say our ancestors were wrong to do that. That they should have had strict immigration laws and deported them when their visas ran out. But traditional Native people all know it had to be as it was. The obligation of hospitality is absolute, and a true human being must follow it. Of course, when the visitor does not know or follow those instructions and abuses that hospitality his host no longer has that obligation.

When the Pilgrims landed on Cape Cod their first act was to steal the winter food supplies of the local village. Then they sailed across the bay to the site of Patuxet, a village that was now empty because the inhabitants had all succumbed to a white man's disease. Ousemequin, the massasoit or great leader of the Wampanoag, sent people to greet and assist those Pilgrims. They helped them to survive that first hard winter (the Pilgrims had arrived in <u>November</u>!) and to teach them about making the maple sugar, and trapping the herring when they ran to the sea in early spring. They taught them how to plant the three sisters, corn, beans and squash, together in a mound fertilized by a buried fish. They taught which berries were good to eat and which wild plants were medicines. When the English had good harvest in the fall they made a feast, and my ancestors came and brought meat, deer and wild fowl, as were our instructions.

That day is what Americans commemorate in their November holiday of Thanksgiving. Some of our people gather in the Pilgrim's town of Plymouth on that day but call it a Day of Mourning, making speeches to cultivate public awareness of the abuses to Native people and to the earth, not only by the Pilgrims and Puritans in the seventeenth century, but that continue to this day across America.

When I am invited to speak in the schools about our history I tell the children candidly that feast in 1621 was the last good party we had with the Europeans. The story from then on is one of continuous greed, dishonesty, and tyranny on the part of the conquerors. And I tell them when they have their own Thanksgiving feast to remember the hospitality of the Indian and how the English betrayed it. And I tell them that for us Thanksgiving is not just one day a year, but every time our people come together, every time we eat, and every morning when we wake to a new day.

Fifty-four years after that harvest feast, Metacomet, the new massasoit, son of Ousemequin, had enough of the English treachery, cheating, abuse and high-handed treatment of his people. He visited all of our surrounding neighbor nations and tried to convince them to join with him and drive the invaders back to their own lands. By then it was too late. (Probably too late by a hundred and fifty years – if the Arawak and Carib people had not followed the instruction of hospitality but had sunk Columbus when he first landed, it might have put off the invasion for a while. But not long enough for our people to be prepared for the unexpected inhumanity of the European invaders.) By then there were English towns everywhere. They had been converting many Indian villages to Christianity, and none of these "praying Indians", as they were called, would stand with Metacomet against the invaders. The numbers were against him when the war broke out, and he and his allies fought bravely for a year and a half but were finally defeated. Metacomet and the other leaders were all killed, their heads displayed on poles around Plymouth town, and their families sold into slavery in the West Indies.

Similar stories were repeated over and over during the conquest of Turtle Island by the European adventurers. The invaders would be welcomed in friendly fashion by the inhabitants, feasted and gifted and proclaimed to be relatives in ceremonies. Agreements were made and treaties were signed, all of which were honored by the Indians. All of which were broken by the Europeans.

Was it wrong, was it foolish to follow our instruction of hospitality? I don't think it was. Looking back we see that a teeming population of oppressed people would invade this beautiful continent and push us out of the way. It was inevitable, given their culture and circumstances. We fought when we had to, but we held on to our Original Instructions. We were the true human beings caring for the land and our children.

It is important for us to understand that and not forget our instructions now. If we follow our instructions as the elders taught we will live and we will not be conquered. When we forget and take on the ways of the invaders, the ways of greed and selfishness, of arrogance and badmouthing, of deception and dishonesty, then we have truly lost and we no longer live.

It is very simple, really. You don't have to understand or believe in the Original Instructions. But you want to be happy. Don't you? Doesn't everyone? It shouldn't be hard to understand that happiness requires there not be continual fear and stress. Happiness blooms when there is harmony, just as flowers bloom when there is warmth and a balance of sun and rain.

As human beings we have learned that survival is easier when we cooperate and care for each other, and that caring is also the greatest source of joy. We have learned that cooperation and caring require trust, and so trust is the essential ingredient of all relationship. It is for our benefit that we learn to create the trust that makes our relationships, our families and communities, safe and welcoming to every person. We create that safety by adhering to mutual respect, living in a circle of equals, with gratitude, humility, honesty, generosity, awareness, courage, and humor.

Hospitality is the policy which allows for our safe travel through the world, for our leaning of other people and other ways, and coming close to them, opening our hearts as well as our minds further, for adding to our sense of the inherent goodness of human beings and all of Creation.

What it comes down to is this: there once was a world where people huddled close to the fire and each other against the cold without, and cared lovingly for one another with great concern for those too young, too old, or too weak to care for themselves. Yes, there was such a world, believe me, for I have lived with its vestiges and helped in their renewal, and in many small and remote parts of the earth it still survives

But most of the world today, the ninety nine percent that you and I inhabit, is a world of separate, lonely individuals struggling to survive unaided, the great majority hungry every day of their lives, without adequate shelter or medical care, the rest storing up material goods and personal wealth against their restless discontent and terrors of a lonely life and death without meaning. This is a world of escalating selfishness, greed, violence and fear. A world of locked doors, prisons, police, and attack dogs, television and computer surveillance, and weapons of mass destruction being sold for great profit to all nations, to the military and non-military terrorists and criminals.

That is the world we live in today in the first decade of the twenty-first century, shorn of its beauty by ugly constructions and pollution. That is the hell to which we were banished when this civilization arose from the misled mind of man to devour us all. Whether the world that was, that came before the rise of civilization ten thousand years ago, was a paradise is a matter of conjecture, a matter of taste and definition. But it did not have the features named above from which we all suffer today.

So which will you choose? A world of locks and jails, of walls and cages, where rules are more important than people, laws more important than justice, protection more important than compassion, comfort more important than kindness, or a world where we are responsible for each other, where hands are for healing and soothing and caressing, not for killing and hurting. Where children laugh, and we laugh with them. Where we all live inside each other's eyes.

That world is the only safe world. The safety that grows from mutual agreements. The Original Instructions suggest that through our adherence to the universal obligation of hospitality we can be at home anywhere on our Mother Earth, with any people, and the safety and trust of each fire will be the same for all our human family.

Locks, guards, suspicion, coldness, fear. Or openness, generosity, welcoming, smiles, warmth, love. Put it that way, it's clear what choice any reasonable human being would make. But it cannot be that simple, you say. Well – I think it is. Just so simple. That makes me a radical, I guess, an idealist anyway. But, you know, I have experienced both worlds. I see that human beings are capable of both modes of being, of both ways of acting.

The fear and mistrust, the greed and selfishness, are not natural to human beings. They are taught to people by the way they are treated, taught to children by the models of the adults, taught and reinforced by their culture. Indigenous people living apart from the dominant culture, preserving older traditions of living as equals closely with one another, are naturally hospitable and helpful. For an untroubled human being it is normal and ordinary to be helpful. Millions of years of tribal living and evolution around cooperation and helpfulness have placed that firmly in our inheritance. The open human heart knows that happiness resides, not in taking and holding to ourselves, but in giving and being helpful to others.

This is a human being instruction, as my elders said, and not an Indian teaching. My elders knew this, but so did yours, a long time ago, and so do many still around the world in many cultures. Marshall Rosenberg writes of his grandmother, a poor woman raising nine children, who never turned anyone from her door. When she fed one ragged beggar who was homeless she gave him a place to stay the night and he stayed seven years! This was normal for a woman who never asked who you were, only what you needed.

Things to think about: Ask yourself, what is my reaction when people visit unexpectedly, without invitation? What am I thinking? What do they really want or need? Do they feel welcome? How do I make them feel comfortable and at home? It is probable that, even though they may not realize it themselves, what they really need is a sympathetic listener.

The elders I knew so long ago opened their homes to me, shared whatever they had, and treated me like an honored guest and a long-lost member of the family they were so happy to be with. I did contribute whatever they would allow me to, and I never felt like a stranger, but that it was so completely natural for us to be together there.

If we would choose a world in which human beings are trusting, kind, caring, and generous, then I suppose it is up to us to act accordingly. To be the ones who take the first steps to turn it all around. To practice, as the bumper stickers tell us, "random acts of kindness." Perhaps the great revolution that turns civilization around and makes it human begins just inside our own doors, which are open, where the warm glow of hospitality invites all the world to come in. "Mi casa, su casa!"

HOSPITALITY

Come in, come in, they say,
Let's get acquainted. Take that chair,
It's more comfortable. Coffee
Or tea – how do you like it?
Where are you from, then?
Never met anyone from there before.
Your people got any good stories?

Kids filling the windows and the door,
They're all curious – well, sure,
If you don't mind the bunch of them,
Come on, kids, come on in.
How about songs? Can you sing some?
You gotta stay now, it's too late
To go anywhere tonight , right?

Hot soup and laughter, acceptance,
Curiosity. Call the neighbors in, life
Reflected from many eyes, everybody
Just shares what's on the stove.
And that's your room there –
We'll tell stories, sing some songs.
Just slip away when you're tired,
We'll let you sleep in the morning.

Recognize that scene? I know it
From years of visits to hundreds
Of homes in Indian North America,
But I could imagine it also
In just about any simple humble
Home of poor working or peasant
People in any village around the world.

The only place I can't image
Such openness, connection and sharing
Is in the great mansions of the wealthy
Or the comfortable, insured, legally
Protected, gentrified apartments
And three bedroom houses with lawns
Of the white collar upwardly mobile
With gates security monitored and policed.

Blind behind shuttered systems we see
Not the fruits and folly of dominion.

PART FOUR

DIRECTION: WEST – Connecting with Spirit

ELEMENT WATER

Three personal instructions to make life easier and more rewarding,
or

CREATION IS PURELY JOY

PART FOUR – WEST

For the last direction of the west, and the three instructions I have chosen for our contemplations concerning the spirit, I have decided to bring us to the western edge of Turtle Island. Again we are on a beach (I spent much of my childhood on Massachusetts beaches and am always drawn to these places where my imagination may fly over the oceans to all those strange shores across the world).

This beach, in the northwest of Turtle Island, at the far north of the Olympic peninsula, is the land of the Makah people. Like my own Wampanoag people, they are people of the sea, people who have traditionally found their survival setting forth in canoes into the mysterious and changeable ocean. Like our old tribes on Nantucket Island, these seamen found a large part of their subsistence hunting the whale. Today they have returned to this practice to help revive their old traditional ways and make them strong again as a people.

This in spite of opposition from 'Save the Whale' groups, in my opinion a misplaced opposition. The enemy is not a small tribe keeping themselves together by a few regulated ritual whale hunts in canoes that set forth prayerfully from here in Neah Bay in a sacred manner. These people should not be opposed, but held up as examples of right livelihood in relationship to conservation and the environment The enemy is greed and the unregulated industries in countries that continue to plunder and reduce the world's whale populations beyond sustainability.

Of course, on Turtle Island we could go further west by going north to Alaska and west to the Aleutians, but I am only taking us to places where I have personally been so that I have them clearly in mind as we sit and talk together. As I look west from here there is only the great Pacific Ocean, and in my imagination all those islands of Polynesia and Melanesia discovered by our intrepid ancestors setting out with incredible courage in outrigger canoes towards a vast empty horizon. I think of the Maori, many of whom I have met, whose people also were whale hunters.

The instructions we will consider to enhance our spiritual understanding and connection seem to be very appropriate to our apprehension of this vast ocean and the adventures of our relatives that found and populated its lovely islands. The instructions I have chosen for this direction are Wisdom, Courage, and Beauty.

10. WISDOM

Knowledge is of the past; wisdom is of the future.

So runs an old Native proverb

Wisdom. Is that teachable? Maybe not, but it is learnable. I am supposed to be passing along to you the wisdom of the elders. What I can remember that the old ones told me when I was younger. So here is what they always told me when I asked them how I could get to be as wise as they: "Make a lot of mistakes."

In which case I should be pretty wise by now, with all the mistakes I've made in eight decades. But we don't always learn from our mistakes right away. Some of us are a little slow.

Still that's the only method I can recommend, clumsy as it is, if you're looking for a method. There are things you can notice that help, though. Coming under the instruction of Awareness. We can also pay attention to the mistakes others make. Knowledge is good. We need plenty of it to manage our lives in the complicated world we have to navigate. It's useful and necessary to learn how things work, and to learn about the past, in order that we be not, as Santayana said, condemned to repeat its mistakes. But the future has limitless choices for us, and since we are all heading into the future every moment, we must also be concerned with wisdom.

My pal Slow Turtle used to have a sign on his desk that read, "Ignorance is curable, Stupidity isn't." Perhaps with that he hoped to intimidate a few visitors out of asking so many stupid questions. (He was, among many other things, the Director of the Commission on Indian Affairs for the Commonwealth of Massachusetts.) Stupidity, if it's not the opposite of ignorance, is it the opposite of wisdom? Might be worth looking at.

Because if we are stupid, then Creation has made us that way. And if Creation is interested in evolution, and it seems to be, then it must intend for us to get un-stupid. There must be a way in Creation for human beings to become wise. Most of us blame ourselves for being stupid, and most of us would like to become wise.

Well, I don't think it's helpful to blame ourselves for being stupid, and it's not much better to blame Creation for that. Maybe by now, if you've listened to the kind of thinking I've been sharing, you realize that where I place the blame is on the kind of social structure that we have inherited and contend with in the world of today.

Here's why.

115

For one thing, I really think most of us are not as wise as we were when we were newborns. There is a wisdom in human nature that was part of the equipment Creation installed in us, which the cultures we are born in try to knock out of us as soon as possible.

Those questioning looks babies give us sometimes – I don't think they are asking what to do; I think they are trying to figure out why we grown-ups do such dumb things. Like running around all upset, raising our voices, getting stern, cold, pre-occupied, unfriendly, anxious, depressed. Getting angry, fighting. Babies are perhaps trying to figure out if these things are fun for us. They don't quite get what's the pleasure we have in them, but we must be enjoying ourselves, otherwise why would we do them?

I have made a study in my life observing newborns and very young infants. I have noticed things that I think are important for us to consider. When babies arrive in this life they are very glad to be here. For some it was an easy birth and they are ready to move on and see where they are to plug in to this world. Or perhaps they had a hard time getting here, the pregnancy and the birth may have been difficult, dangerous even, perhaps painful and terrifying. But once this transition is over and discharged into the past, all babies seem very excited about being alive and very interested in this new and expanded environment.

They are not confused about what they are doing here. They are not anxious to find their identity or discover what their role is. They see right away that their job is to explore everything and learn as much about it as they can. They follow avidly the Original Instruction of Awareness.

Have you ever seen a bored or disinterested newborn? I haven't. They may be curious, excited, laughing, crying, or just quietly contemplating. But they are never bored, never depressed. They don't worry about what will happen, they just stay in the moment and follow what is going on. They are taking it all in.

Doing that can be a lot of fun, as things must be observed and handled and tasted and thrown and so on, in the pursuit of knowledge. What they seek, it seems, is how to use the world around them. Sometimes it is to eat, and of course that's important. But what they really are looking for, it seems, is how to play with it.

What they come here fully equipped for is to play. There is not a concept of past or future. There is only this moment, and this moment, if we are fed, rested, and comfortable, is for having fun.

So I think another method for becoming wise could be, if you are open-minded and observant, just to hang out with babies. If you are willing to be taught, they will teach you. Of course life is supposed to be fun. Their question for you is how you will relate together, how can you have fun together. 'Come, let's play,' their expressions often say. If you can enter into that with them it is pure joy and hilarity for them.

Because although the material world can be a lot of fun even when no one else is around, what they really want is a partner in play. There is no joy like joy shared and the games our creativity can invent together can escalate our elation of the partnership moment by moment into sheer ecstasy.

This wisdom of babies is surely worth considering. First, that the world is a marvelous and exciting place. A source of endless study and interest. Second, that life is to be lived enthusiastically, moment to moment, and its purpose is to have fun. Third, and very important, is that other creatures are even more wonderful than material things, and the best thing about them is how we can relate together. Whether the other creature is an animal or a human being, large or small, it is best if we can touch and be close and communicate, with eyes, facial expressions, sounds, hands, bodies and minds.

All of us started life with this wisdom. Very soon things begin to happen to us, however, that make us doubt ourselves and our own wisdom. People begin to act strangely with us. They are not always fun, and they are not always friendly. Sometimes they act indifferent, distracted, pre-occupied, uncaring, cold or angry. They act judgmentally. They act as if we were not always wonderful and loveable beings.

We begin to doubt them or ourselves or both. We start to react differently. We become shy or aggressive, we feel shame, we hide our true feelings. We lose our spontaneous trusting expression of who we are and what we feel. We learn to create acceptable masks and protective armor.

Life gets harder, more complicated, without close allies, without support or explanation. We have to find our own way through all this and somehow survive. The sense that life is supposed to be fun begins to erode slowly. We learn we can trust people only so far, and some not at all, that life is a struggle and only rarely is it fun so we must not expect too much of it.

We call our desire for life to be fun unrealistic, childish. We keep hoping there will be someone who we can relate to with complete closeness and understanding and trust, but little by little this hope fades and we understand we must settle for relationships that are a bit superficial, a bit distant, but safe from attack and injury. We abandon hope for a rich and joyful life of fun and passion and settle for getting by. This wisdom of newborns has been forgotten as though we never had it.

That's why I say watching babies and young children can be a wonderful teaching. But only if we abandon the arrogance that believes them to be ignorant and really consider the wisdom they have brought with them from Creation. It is instructive to watch the changes they go through as the changes of the years.

When Emmy Rainwalker and I opened our home to be an annex of our town's day care center. I loved being with and interacting with the young ones. Very quickly I began to notice the various kinds of patterns of behavior, and I played a little game in my mind imagining the kind of home each must have, the kind of parents and how they related to their children. Then at the end of the day when the parents came to pick up their children I could see that my surmises were very closely born out.

I have two homes. In New Hampshire we live in the woods and watch birds and animals through my windows. In Copenhagen we live beside the playground of a day care center. I sit in the morning and have breakfast watching the little ones at their play. It's a wonderful way to start the day. It's a daily reminder of how wonderful we human beings really are. But the lessons of the hazards of the culture are also there to observe. The various aggressions of a few, the anxieties, the shyness, the manipulations, the seductions, the confusions, you can see them all in their early operation. The budding sexism, the tractability or rebelliousness. Little by little the culture is changing and reforming them through their parents, siblings, friends and teachers, and this will continue and get stronger as they grow through their school years.

I want to keep guiding them, to keep guiding myself and all of us, back to the pure wisdom of Creation we all knew when we were newborns. So I recommend trying often to put in some quality alone time with very new little babies. Return their intense gaze with a smile of reassurance that you are really there now and allow yourself to make a deep connection with a wise one.

There is another kind of wisdom that we do not usually discover until we have grown quite old. That is the wisdom of <u>patience</u>. Perhaps we do not need that quality when we are newborns, because there is nothing but the present moment, and it is so full. A baby is never bored. What is there involves her so fully she has no time to wish for more and has no expectations. Everything seems to be quite enough. But after a while it seems we begin to long for other things, people, experiences we have tasted and miss or discover to exist but don't have. Dissatisfaction sets in. We want <u>more</u>. And we want it now. Impatience sets in, and we struggle with that most of our lives while everything is not as we want it to be.

Which is all right. It keeps things moving forward. "What do we want?" we cry. "Peace!" we respond. "When do we want it?"... "Now!" As well we should. There is much in this world that needs fixing, that should not exist in this age. War. Violence. Hunger. Poverty. Lack of housing, medical care, education, for most of the people on the planet. We cannot be satisfied being warm and well fed while others are cold and hungry. The young get impatient with their elders sometimes for seeming to accept what is intolerable. And it is good that they do.

But now I am older, and I have discovered that patience is a great quality which I had not truly experienced in my youth. I see now that it is an instruction given primarily to elders to maintain a good balance in the councils of human beings. I consider this instruction so valuable that originally I thought of naming this chapter "Patience",

But after more reflection I realized that patience is but one part of that gem we call wisdom, which everyone seeks and which has many facets. I want to ask you to consider it here and to keep the instruction handy to balance your own impatience, which can lead you astray.

I can never recall any of the old people talking about patience. When as young people we displayed our impatience with this or that, they said nothing. They did not sigh, they did not restrain us, they did not turn away or glance knowingly at each other. They only smiled.

Something in that smile to give one pause. Elders are to learn from. Is this a teaching? If I am impatient and this old one only smiles perhaps there is something I do not understand. Or. Perhaps he does not understand. The need. The urgency. The consequences. Perhaps I should explain more. He listens. And smiles. What am I to make of this?

The elders, as I have noted before, rarely verbalize teachings in direct pronouncements. About respect, yes, and often. About the circle, of course, and what it means. And probably in our young lives at least once about the instructions of Awareness, Generosity, Hospitality. But they never preached. Just a bit of information that could help a child on the path to being a human being. What that means. To be a man or a woman of ones family, tribe or clan, what it means to travel the good red road in a sacred manner.

The other instructions, Thanksgiving, Honesty, Humor, Humility, Courage, Beauty, would, like Patience, become apparent mainly through stories, and through teasing and joking And most of all, by example. The best teachers were the embodiment in themselves, in their lives, in their actions and re-actions, of the Original Instructions. Many old ones did not seem to think of themselves as teachers. Their business was to learn and accordingly to live their lives in the best way possible. That was their business. Your business was also to learn, and if you watched and listened and paid good attention you would do that. It was up to you.

I have saved patience to put in until now because it leavens all the others. We will probably not live up to every instruction fully every moment of our lives. We are probably going to slip and stumble occasionally. We want always to be what creation has intended, full human beings. But things happen to us, we pick up bad habits and patterns, and often we disappoint ourselves. That's when we need to remember that smile of our elders. It's all right. Be patient. Sometimes it's like this. Hang on. Smile.

I can't remember any wise sayings about Patience from the elders. Probably there were stories that I've forgotten – sometimes age tricks you like that. But the instruction was there for us always.

The patience the old ones taught we could only learn by paying attention to how they lived their lives. But if I want to be really complete in my passing on what I have learned about the Original Instructions, I need somehow to convey to you in words what I have not ever heard in so many words. Because the older I get the more I understand about patience.

Patience will give us a chance to correct any disrespect we may have shown. Patience lets us work through the hard and stuck places in our relationships. When we forget to be aware, to be generous, to be hospitable, to give thanks, be honest, humble or brave, patience gives us forgiveness and reminds us that we are more happy and more human when we remember and follow our Original Instructions.

Looking back again, as we have been during these reflections, it looks like we human beings were fairly patient before we got swallowed up in this impatient civilization. Life progressed slowly for us. The ones we call Homo Sapiens spread themselves out over thousands of years, out of Africa and up through Europe and across Asia. Then maybe 70-100,000 years ago Homo Sapiens Sapiens came along and for a while both Neanderthal and modern human beings co-existed at the same time but separately, it seems. Perhaps some may have joined with the newer people, but if so it seems they were unable to produce offspring, and after a while the older species just disappeared.

Nothing much speeded up after that, though. Tens of thousands of years went by without big changes. In spring, life stirred in the earth, blossoms and leaves appeared, fish ran in the swollen rivers, newborn animals were venturing from their nests, and men and women emerged from their community shelters to cooperate in the hunting, fishing, and gathering of wild foods. Summer arrived bearing fresh berries and fruits as well as root plants, and people ranged further in the hunt, went to the sea to harvest its many comestibles. And then autumn and the salting, smoking and putting away of foods for the confining winter months. Year after year went by, the seasons turning ever in the steady pace of the earth around the sun. Hundreds of turnings, thousands, tens of thousands.

You and I, living then, would see life the same from birth to death, living as our parents, grandparents, and ancestors from before. In such living there could be no impatience. Everything took the time it took. You can't hurry the herring run, the coming of the strawberry. We would watch the new sprouts of grass in spring rising every day to full waist-high depths in midsummer. We would wonder together how long it had taken for the mountains to grow to their sizes. And we would notice the even trek of the stars' parade above us night after night, the moon moving among them, and the shooting stars that darted suddenly out of blackness and vanished again.

Patience. If you live in today's world, with the society and culture of contemporary civilization as your environment, and no doubt if you are reading this in the same era that I am writing them, then you are caught up in stress. That's what I hear all the time from everyone: "I'm so stressed!" And most of that is caused or augmented by time pressure. Everything is in a rush. The society and culture of contemporary civilization is your environment, and no doubt if you are reading this in the same era that I am writing them, then you are caught up in stress. That's what I hear all the time from everyone: "everything is in a rush." "When should this be finished?" we ask, and the answer is always, "yesterday."

Many years ago my wife Ellika attended a conference of alternative-minded women in Copenhagen. A large statuesque tribal woman from West Africa who sailed sedately as a great ship into the room, clad in long white gown and white turban, impressed her. The woman listened to some discussion about how people in Africa are oppressed, then rose to address the group.

"You say we are oppressed," she said with great dignity, "but I think you are more oppressed than we." Now she had everyone's interest. Here was a new point of view.

"Look at your arms," she said, "what do you have on your wrists?" Almost everyone glanced at his or her own wristwatches. Some giggled, some looked puzzled, annoyed, or sad. "There is the instrument of your slavery," she added, "we do not have those and are bound by no such master."

Today she might also ask how many are carrying their mobile phones, electronic palm or laptop computers as well. Go in any public place. People are less and less present, less engaged with other people, less aware of their surroundings. They are all talking on cell phones or sinking their attention into a portable computer.

How often do you say and hear from others, "I have no time for that." There are things we may long to do, but there's never enough time. "Hurry up, can't you? We're late!" We have joined the White Rabbit in his endless race: "I'm late, I'm late!"

So we speed up. A long time ago people learned to tame and ride horses. Human life was altered quite a bit then as hunting, emigrating, and the infringement of peoples upon one another were facilitated and increased somewhat. The slightly increased pace of ordinary life changed after that very little for thousands of years. All the way until the last century it stayed like that. Even though people could light the dark a little with fires and candles, still most human activity confined itself to daylight hours.

121

With the coming of the Industrial Revolution things began to change rapidly for the human family. Engines gave power to trains, ships, then automobiles and airplanes, and the race was on to go faster and faster about the earth. Electricity turned night into day, driving new machines around the clock and providing instant communication over vast distances through telegraph, telephone and radio.

The effect of all this new technology was not to make life easier for people, not to create a more relaxed, worry-free environment. It was to create a hunger for ever-greater speed. To add greater complication of activities and things, with attendant needs and sense of urgency. And to give our lives and our souls over to the acquisition of more material things.

Certain aspects of life have improved with advancing technology. Medical treatment, outstandingly. Now we can address those many disabling diseases that we did not have in former times that were brought on by agricultural contact with animals and by the stresses and environmental degradation of industry. And our awareness and knowledge of ourselves and our situation, the nature of existence, continue to expand exponentially with developing instruments of research and the ability of artificial intelligence to store, locate, and combine information, and our ever-increasing opportunities of reaching out to more and more of each other. To bring our stories, our concerns, our fears and desires, our thoughts and our dreams to everyone, to all of our kind in every corner of the planet we all call home.

This is considerable, and does indeed hold great hope for the future. The fact that I can organize this information with my own thinking added so easily with my word-processor and the machinery exists that can publish and distribute it widely enough for you to be reading all this now – that is a marvel. We can use this technology to put all our best thinking together to stop the destruction and begin to build the world of our common dreams.

But we must slow down to do that. We are hell-bent to consume our life support system and burn ourselves out. Our technology helps us to accelerate that process and race blindly, heedlessly, on into the unseen immolation ahead.

We don't have the answers. None of us. My exhortation for us all to just stop what we are doing and think about it is not a complete answer, obviously. I don't even know how to get everyone to do that much. We have experts who have proposed workable ways for us to stop pollution, and environmental degradation and save the life on earth, to create world peace, to provide basic human needs for all people, to end crime and violence everywhere and transform the perpetrators into valuable community members, to raise children that are kind and caring, curious to learn throughout their lives, happy, playful, and creative. There is no lack of expertise in these areas and stratagems that will work. But we don't know how to initiate them. How to get us all to agree to working together and trying new things.

We are going too fast. Too overloaded. Too much to do, too little time. Here we are in a bind. We have to save the earth. Save the rainforests. Save the endangered species. Save the water. Save the children. Urgently. Yesterday. As the Red Queen said to Alice, we have to keep running faster just to stay in the same place. How do we get off this treadmill?

Patience.

The older I get the greater my patience grows.

If we follow this Original Instruction we can pull back. We can sit still a while and stare off into space. Look, the earth still turns without my assistance. The only thing I really have to do is die, and I don't have to do that just yet.

I can take some time to stop and think. Or stop and not think. Just hang out in the sun and feel the wind, like those chamomile flowers, or the blue chicory over there, or that lizard just dozing on that rock.

As I said, I have no complete answer. I have no prescription. I have no manifesto. Certainly I don't believe in revolution. Look what has happened to all the revolutions, from the American and the French to the Russian and Chinese, to all the Third World revolutions. The Outs get in and throw the Ins out. The rich keep getting richer and more powerful, the poor poorer and weaker.

That's what comes of impatience. They had good causes: liberty, equality, fraternity - justice, and a good life for all. But they didn't take the time to work it out. To talk it over in circles with everyone. Get agreement about the problems and the causes, be open to all ideas, explore and experiment. These revolutions wanted to change the world for a minority. They talked about "the people" but left out women and people of other races and nations than themselves.

A revolution should not explode. It should never be violent. It should be more like evolution, growing organically, taking its own time, nurtured and tended by loving gardeners. You do not go into your garden and tug on the carrots and tell them to grow faster, tell your corn to grow larger and sweeter else they go on the block as traitors to the revolution, You pray and prepare the soil with your best knowledge, plant the seeds, water and fertilize them, then wait and watch. Perhaps you weed and mulch, pick off insects and fence out predators. Your garden takes its own time, and the time it takes depends on many factors. You must only be patient. The harvest for you this year will teach you more for the next year's preparations and planting.

As the giant corporate farms of the agriculture industry produce food that is inferior in quality to that of small organic farmers, food that has lost most of its nutrients but is artificially bloated and colored and poisoned, so also our small human communities are capable of creating a healthy, interesting, creative, and joyous way of life that our huge over-blown nation-states cannot give us. They give us the slogans of freedom, equality, justice, and a decent secure life for all its citizens, but they cannot, and will not deliver the reality of them.

In our gardens, our small communities where we mend the sacred circle of our people, we may put our hearts and minds together to grow a new and better world, a more human world, garden by garden, season by season. We will make mistakes. They are our lessons. We must not be discouraged. We will have successes, lessons too. Year by year we can grow our world. We keep putting our hearts and minds together. To learn what goes well, what could be better. We listen and go on working, singing, helping each other. Playing with the children.

Patience.

We are initially patient when we are babies, I think. Patience is an instruction we are born with, impatience is taught to us. That is why some cultures seem more patient and some more impatient. It's in the culture. If our parents and all around us are patient we do not learn to be impatient.

This life is a whole new experience for a baby. When we are born we had known only the little world of our mother's womb for nine months. Suddenly there is so much to take in, light in our eyes, air in our lungs, many kinds of sounds in our ears. A lot to process. We have no knowledge so no preconceived ideas of how it is supposed to be. No expectations. It is what it is. We accept it, because we know no other.

As a baby we have no concept of time. We have no schedule, no awareness that schedules may exist. When we feel hunger we express it, and if we are uncomfortable we let it be known, and when we are tired we sleep. If our basic needs are met time has no meaning or use for us. If we are not fed or looked after when we are uncomfortable or allowed to sleep when we need it, we will express ourselves more vociferously, becoming more and more insistent until our needs our met. When we have developed the expectation of having our needs met and that expectation is frequently unmet, we will usually develop impatience.

Impatience comes from an expectation that things will not be right unless we complain or take some action to fix them.

Well, it is certainly right to notice the things that are not going well and consider how to improve them. And the economic disaster that America brought on to the whole world with a costly and unnecessary war and a greed that infected the whole business world brought an urgency to the newly elected government. The menace of global warming also is one that needed immediate redressing. These actual threats required attention and action before they got worse. They required of us caution and our best thinking at once. But patience enough not to instill a sense of panic and fear.

It is when we expect things to go wrong that we become impatient.

If we grow up in a culture in which we have been cared for patiently without urgency, without a sense that disaster is lurking everywhere, if all is proceeding in a relaxed, calm atmosphere without great hurry or delay, attuned to the rhythms of life, of day and night and the procession of the seasons, we will have no reason to learn or develop impatience.

We develop impatience in our children when we are impatient with them. We are impatient with them when we have an expectation of them. A "should." We think they "should" know better. We think they "should" have learned by now. We are telling them they are not right, not as they "should" be. "When will you grow up?" we ask. So they become impatient to grow up. They want to do things before they are ready. They are not content with who they are and where they are. They are impatient for it to be different than it is.

As babies we had no thought that anything should be different than it was, as long as we were fed and comfortable and rested. As long as there were people and things to explore and play with. Everything was as it was, and it was all interesting. Everything happened as it happened, and, as long as it was not threatening or scary, that was interesting too. Funny, perhaps. Sometimes hilarious.

That's one of the things wrong with our schooling. We have expectations of children and are impatient with them. We will teach certain things at certain times to all the children, expecting each one will be ready and interested to learn just what we present when we present it. Of course, this is crazy. They are all individuals, growing at different rates, with different backgrounds and different interests. Against their will and inclination, by which they would grow and learn naturally and well, we try to force them to learn, grammar and spelling at nine o'clock, arithmetic at ten o'clock, social studies at eleven – no wonder we never learned well in school, we were bored stiff. If we had any mind left it was out the window with the birds and the clouds. Years and years it took us to learn what we could have learned in a few days if we were really eager to learn it. Look how the children today teach themselves about computers.

Luckily no one tried to teach us to speak. We learned that on our own, before teachers got a hold of us. They could have made the lessons so dull it would have taken us years to be able to talk instead of a few months.

The old way of learning was for children to seek on their own what they wanted to know. They would watch, imitate, ask questions, get shown, try it out and practice until they knew it quickly and well. The old ones waited until the little ones showed an interest before they encouraged or imparted knowledge.

A good storyteller is not impatient to get to the end of the story. She takes the time to engage her listeners, to take them with her on a journey through another world. To tell the climate and the landscape and discover the distinctive features of its characters. She will take time to bring in humor and suspense and surprise. With patience people will want to linger in that story. As when you are nearing the end of a really good book and begin to feel sorry that it will soon be over.

This book has proceeded at its own pace and taken me longer than I thought, but just as long to write as was necessary. I had no expectations ahead of time, nor have I ever. The first book I wrote, <u>Return to Creation</u>, took me twelve years. I had to live it as I was learning and recording it. Each one is different and takes the time it takes to grow. Like children.

Whenever you are feeling impatient I recommend you walk away from the affairs of people for a little while. Walk through a meadow or into the woods. The acorn is not saying to itself, oh, it takes too long to be an oak tree, I want to be a poplar tree, or an ash, or maybe even a dandelion and bloom right away. The maple is not saying, oh, I must get these seeds made quickly and send them on their winged flight. The hills are not saying, will I ever grow to be a mountain? The mountains are not impatient to be worn smooth into hills.

The little spring that rises in the cool dark glade is sometimes spouting laughing water to the creek, and sometimes is dry and silent. The world slows further with the falling snow and all is still and quiet. Then the lake is frozen and the little stream gurgles below shelves of ice. Days grow warmer, snow melts, and the rains soak the earth. Sap is running, and we collect he sweet juice of the maple tree. Soon the buds appear, grow to blossoms and leaves and sweetness fills the breezes of spring, beckoning the long warm days of summer. The grass grows tall and the berries appear to summon the birds and the bears. Once more the chill creeps in the night, frost appears on the meadows and the leaves blush orange and red and yellow, turn brown and settle on the earth for another winter.

The time of life revolves in circles. It does not plunge straight toward some intent or goal as human beings do with an ambition that prods them on a scheduled timetable into the future. It is really difficult to feel and be attuned to the rhythm of life in our cities. Even the parks don't feel so natural— often more museums of nature tended by curators. We have banished Mother Earth under pavements, and we flee from her, from wind and air and sun and weather in our air-conditioned high-rise buildings. We harvest our foods in any season from the super market.

Are we happy so? We don't seem to be, with our high blood pressure and heart trouble and ulcers and cancer and stress related diseases, mental and emotional break-downs, pill-popping, alcohol and drug abuse, our over-eating, workaholic, shopaholic, sexually compulsive, alienated, lonely and violent society.

Listen! There are insects droning in the grass. Little frogs chirping over by that woodland pool. The splash of two otter playing in the beaver pond below. The wind whispering in the grass. Conversations of the birds in the bushes.

We're not even listening to each other. We'd better. That's the only thing that can save us.

We used to do it.

When we were living in that cave, remember? All of us together, grandparents, parents, children. After a day of gathering wild food and hunting, preparing the food to eat, skins to wear. Sitting around the fire listening to the stories of the day's activities, the questions of the little ones, the remembering of the old ones, the planning for the morrow. We listened carefully to each one. We shared our thinking, our problems, our fears, our dreams.

When the circle grew to a village, and we all had family houses, we built a big round house where we could come together. To dance. To sing, to tell stories. To listen. To decide and to do together what was decided.

Remember?

It was like that. I remember. Do you? We weren't stressed, or confused, because we followed a path we had followed since time before memory. We didn't have to struggle alone. We had our people, and it was "one for all and all for one." Life was secure and good, and we knew who we were and where we belonged.

Today, after ten thousand years of civilization we are no longer secure. We entrust our safety to the government, but governments are often scary too. Terrorists have us nervous, looking over our shoulders, photographed by security cameras, going through metal detectors everywhere we go. People are struggling and stressed, feeling isolated and having little or no support. Many of us are single parents with no one to help care for our children, and we can't be there for them because we have to work to feed and house them. And even if some of us are living together in couples, we often must both go out to work, and sometimes work overtime or moonlight with another job, because we can't afford to pay all the bills. The food the house, the clothes, the car, the gas, the oil the electricity, the insurance, the taxes, the credit cards for all the stuff we bought. Books for the kids' school. Taking the kids to school, to soccer, shopping. Work around the house. Telephone. Email. The doctor. The dentist. Keep moving. No time to stop. Maybe when we're dead.

You don't remember how it was, so long ago? I'll remind you. We rose in the morning when the sky got light, when the birds began to call. We ate and talked together about what there was to do and who would be doing what. We cleaned and prepared our tools and weapons for the day's work. Some of us might go hunting. Some might fish. Some might collect berries and herbs or dig for shellfish on the shore. Some might stay with the sick or the very old ones who could not venture out. At the end of the day we would have many stories to tell at our feast. While the sun slept we could too, with the roof of stars to guard our dreaming.

We might seek our food for a few days and prepare and store it in those same days. Then for some days we might only fix up our camp and spend some time making things and repairing things. Making them beautiful.

There was plenty of time. Time to sit and gossip and to joke. To listen to the old ones tell stories. To learn new songs and to dance. To wander by ourselves. To sit by a stream and watch the salmon leap and the bears coming down to catch them. To collect and braid the sweet grass. To play with the babies. To flirt and tease with a new beloved. To make love on a moon-washed shore. Yes, we had time then, long ago. All the time of our lives.

Things to think about: Imagine you have come to the end. You are on your death-bed, and you are reviewing your life. What do you think about the things that were most important? Do you regret you didn't move faster, rise higher, get more stuff done? What was all the rush about? Did you notice that your children, your loved ones, wanted to spend more time with you? Did you feel connected? Were you satisfied just to be you? Breathe, right now, take a breath. There's time still. You have all the time there is. Feel the beauty. This is a wonderful moment.

How shall we recover our lost time? Take one moment now. Stop reading and just breathe. Listen. There, you took some time back. That's a start. Beginning to slow down. Maybe you could get another one to join you and sit together. Just look at each other. In silence. Breathe and smile.

It's not so easy. We are conditioned. On the run. Can't stop. Don't have time. So you don't feel comfortable in this silence. You need to fill it. To say something, make the time useful. This is useful. Hush. Take you time. Take your lost time back – it's yours.... you have all the time there is.

And then perhaps one of you will speak finally out of the fullness of that silence. Take the time to listen. Don't answer. Don't respond in your mind. Just listen. Take it in. A relationship is deepening here. And lives grow richer.

How much happier and healthier people would be if they simplified their lives. Radically. Gave up all the stuff that clutters and dominates their lives, and their big houses to hold it. How much more satisfying to build your own house, raise your own food, weave your own clothes, make your own music, together with your neighbors, to work with them and play with your children together, tell and listen to your own stories together. To celebrate together, make ceremonies together, and bring the rhythms of our lives to a human tempo. Not to settle for superficial titillation, but to explore the deepest pleasures of beauty and love together.

And sometimes to go to the mountain top alone, to walk the shore by oneself and listen to the ancient voices of the sea from whence we came, and to look up to the stars and the slow spiraling of the galaxy through the expanding orb of the universe.

Then we may attune ourselves, as when we were born, to the patience of Creation.

ELDERS

Grandchildren, beloved seekers,
It's getting late and I have
So much to tell you, do stop,
Only listen. It goes so fast.
The precious moments dropping
Through our hands unheeded.
There's another one, grab it,
Hold on, squeeze it, taste it,
Love it, don't keep looking
For another one, like Faust.
This is the one, the perfect now.
This is forever, only now-
Listen! The wind. The grass.
The sun. The birds. The hearts
Pressed so briefly to ours.

Elders, all of you gone now
From this life, come to me,
I could listen forever
Remembering some small parts
Of all you tried to tell me,
Needing to pass on the gifts
You gave me to all the lovers,
The seekers and the children.
For now I am the elder so
Strange it is to accept
But your love still glows in me,
Your humor, patience, faith,
Make clear the path and possible.

So, beloved lovers and seekers,
Listen well, it goes faster,
Faster, faster, faster,
Only stop, embrace and listen
The elders' hearts in me beat
For you, and my love may
Glow in you when I'm gone,
Making the path clearer
                    and possible

130

11. COURAGE: THE WARRIOR CODE

The teaching of courage is the basis of so many tales of the people that it gives us a sense of how important this instruction is for human beings. Even though our elders never really told us we must be brave. They showed it with their lives. And in the stories they told. In those stories acts of cowardice were ridiculed and acts of courage were praised. They never told us, "don't be afraid". They understood fear is natural to all beings. They said it's all right to feel afraid, just don't let it stop you. It's not courage if you aren't afraid. It's courage when you are scared but go on anyway.

Courage was so highly regarded that many of our ancestors devised ways to test the courage of their enemies and honored them greatly when they proved themselves. But courage does not only mean physical bravery and stamina. To face death with honor was easier than facing disapproval and dishonor.

Courage means doing the right thing. Sometimes that's easy, but most often it is not. For instance, if someone attacks you, should you fight? Maybe not. Maybe everyone thinks you should fight, maybe they won't understand if you don't, maybe everyone will think you are weak. A coward. But maybe you are more brave in not fighting. Maybe you can see it will make things worse. Then it takes a lot of courage not to fight.

There have been sometimes in my life when I have fought and that has made things better, brought more understanding. But there have also been many times when I have fought and it has made things worse. Although I always seek peace, I have also always had the warrior nature that wants to set things right. Sometimes it's hard to know what is the right way. The pressure of others' opinions is not a good guide. We need the courage to stand alone and think and act on our beliefs.

We need the courage to question our own beliefs. Where did they come from? Have we unquestioningly accepted the belief systems of our parents, our peers, our community, our nation, our society? When we are young that is all we know. But at some point in our maturing it is necessary for our own integrity and also for the good of the progress of life and the spirit in Creation, that we extend the range of our thought to go beyond the understanding of our family and friends, our community and nation, to take a wide view of society in the world, of the earth and all life and the progress of the spirit through time.

Human civilization is now at such a point in its history when true courage should be examined. For thousands of years bravery has been measured by going into battle, by man's capacity for violence. The written history of human affairs

131

has been one of violence, of endless war and conquest, of the rise and collapse of empires.

But this does not mean that human nature is fundamentally violent and rapacious. For a much longer time, for over a million years, the circles of human community lived in peace with one another generally and in basic harmony with their environment. Only certain areas of the world developed personal greed and the violence that arises to gratify that greed.

Peaceful peoples cannot remain peaceful under the threat of violence. They must either become violent and follow the ways of war themselves, or be conquered and enslaved. So it was that the violent and greedy nations became empires and proceeded to conquer the peaceful people who lived harmoniously with each other and with nature.

So now there are no nations on earth that do not teach their children greed as a fundamental value and violence as the way to sustain and protect it. That is their religion, no matter what words they use to pray or what art or ritual they practice to cover it and distract themselves. Not by their proclamations, but by their acts you may know them.

The twentieth century saw greater cries for peace than ever before, but its wars were the most horrific in history. After the first Great War in Europe the world was supposed to be made "safe for democracy". But that didn't happen because the victorious nations in their greed did not have the courage to help the defeated, who in their desperation returned to violence again.

World War II was supposed to have been the war to end war. A United Nations Organization was supposed to keep the peace. But the nations had not the courage to truly support it, and other foolish and destructive wars of greed and power ensued in Korea, Vietnam, and Iraq. The people, the nations and their leaders had not the courage to transcend old conventions to interrupt blatant inhumanity and immorality and stop the violence of the Nazis against Jews, Gypsies, communists, homosexuals, people with disabilities and other minorities. They still have not had the will to intervene in warfare between opposing religious, ethnic or tribal groups.

Meanwhile the world is generally unaware that the way to peace had been found and followed for hundreds of years by the Houdenousonie, the People of the Longhouse, called the Iroquois or the Six Nations, in North America. These people had the courage and the wisdom to commit themselves to solving international disputes without war. They declared that henceforward for all time they would resolve their conflicts with words and not weapons. Weapons of war were buried forever. These nations meet every year, following the instructions of the ancient Peacemaker, to sort out all their differences.

Neither weapons nor the threat of violence is allowed in the circles and deliberations of this League of the Great Peace. The fact is the appearance of weapons or the threat of violence would be considered an act of cowardice not of courage in this assembly.

The attacks on the World Trade Center in New York and the Pentagon in Washington in the early part of the new century were considered acts of bravery and righteousness by the perpetrators. Most of the world thought them acts of viciousness and insanity, and for a while the world was truly sympathetic and grieving for the American losses.

But when the American president diverted from pursuit of the criminals to attack an unrelated nation for spurious reasons, the sympathy of most of the world turned against him and he was adjudged to be a bully with suspect political motives. But it would have taken more courage to admit the failure to find Osama bin Laden and continue on the course to bring him and his fellow criminals to justice. Instead the president chose to divert his country's wealth, military power, and attention from that failure by creating and attacking another enemy.

Perhaps it will prove to be important that for the first time in history a massive protest arose around the world <u>before</u> the war began. Perhaps the world will one day become conscious that the traditional response of violence in international conflict is not the path of courage. It is the easy way, the old way, and it should become clear to the world that war has never created peace. That, as Gandhi says, there is no way to peace, peace <u>is</u> the way. But it takes much more courage to bury the hatchet than to pick it up.

Courage. It is a quality we call upon throughout our lives. Not just in moments of great danger, but in the little threats that assault us from all sides in the daily struggle to survive in an unfriendly society. As human beings we are kind and caring, and we continually rise to heights of human courage when challenged. Every day the news brings us stories of ordinary people, as well as police and fire-fighters and emergency medical people risking their lives to save strangers, babies, children, the injured and elderly from accidents, fires, explosions, drowning. My brother, Raven, likes to remind us that every second we breathe there are thousands of people everywhere performing little acts of kindness and thoughtfulness.

There are many times, however, when we must consciously summon our courage. To acknowledge our mistakes, for instance. It takes so much courage to admit when we are wrong. To apologize when we have wronged another – especially our children. To discuss sex, or drugs, with our children when they need our information and support, before they get that from the distressed culture. All the places where it is hard to speak or act, yet we know that it is the right thing, require us to marshal our courage.

The structure of the dominant cultures in the world today creates inequality and isolates people from each other. It glorifies the individual, but only the individual who has the strength of will, the talent and the cunning to survive. To survive in those cultures it helps to be ruthless. It helps immensely for that individual to inherit wealth from strong and ruthless forebears. Survival is thought of in strictly individual terms, although a successful person is also expected to care for her children and other close relatives. In the struggle to survive and be a success, the only reason a person might not lie, cheat, steal, or use force to gain his ends is the fear of getting caught, of being prosecuted and punished. That is hardly a victory for morality. It is, on the contrary, an indication of a depraved culture, rotten and decaying in its very foundations.

The only motive that is truly moral is compassion. Kindness, the love of all Creation and therefore of oneself and all beings. The dominant cultures do not support compassion. They threaten every one of their participants every moment of every day of their lives. The fears generated by those constant and various threats destroy compassion at the same time as they engender selfishness and greed.

It feels like we are weakening ourselves when we admit we are wrong.

We are so invested in being right, we feel if we are not right or if we make a mistake we are less than a person. But actually the admission that we have been wrong makes us much more of a person, gives us far greater stature, although at the time it is hard to see it that way. Marshall Rosenberg, teacher of Non-violent Communication, asks us, do we want to be right, or do we want to be helpful? I think that is a powerful and insightful question, and I try to remember it. Of course it is much more important to be helpful, and insisting on being right is not helpful.

Enforcement of the law involves a lot of courage, and I have nothing but respect and commendation for the police and the soldiers who face grave dangers to enforce the laws of their states and nations. But that does not mean the policies of the courts or of the legislatures are moral.

The law is not compassionate, and that's the problem with the law. The law is not moral. We regard love, compassion, and actions that come from the heart and not the mind as weak, foolish, and dangerous. And yet most of the world's people and religions agree that love is the supreme morality, compassion the supreme dictate. So you see, our notion of justice is not moral, because true morality comes from the heart. Justice, as embodied in the law, has to do with balancing scales, with punishment and retribution, totally immoral concepts, which are central to its functioning.

So now you are probably asking, how can we have justice without law? I can give you an example. After all most of our people lived well, morally and justly, on this continent before our conquest by Europe with all its immoral laws. There has been, in a limited way, a return to the concepts of justice not prescribed by any law except the human heart. There exist today alternative sentencing circles, especially in Canada, arising from cases involving First Nations peoples whose tradition is the Circle (capitalized because considered sacred by them). These sentencing Circles originated in cases of Native people committing crimes within the jurisdiction of their own people, who decided to eschew the judge-and-punish system and to return through a traditional Circle to the tribal ways of community decisions.

In the climate of opinion today it took both understanding and courage to press for the incorporation of these circles. This idea, and the success of its application, was taken up by others interested in restorative justice and community healing. African Americans are now finding that Circles build solidarity and a stronger sense of community, and I can imagine them being effective tools of healing for any people with an identity that is cultural or of a common locality. Such Circles are valuable not only for sentencing, but in other areas of concern, such as drug abuse, domestic violence, dealing with youthful offenders and troubled children. Bringing communities together like this supports everyone, professionals in education, law, and social work, as well as parents and young people.

If you want to learn more about this experiment I can recommend the book Peacemaking Circles, by Pranis, Stuart and Wedge. This book should be a basic text in every law school and required reading for all people involved professionally in the pursuit of justice, from police and social workers to judges and legislators.

This process can heal families devastated by the effects of crime and violence and bring a devastated community close to each other. But more than that, the principles and experiences detailed here used among many groups and for many purposes could inspire and inform every citizen wishing to rebuild a true sense of community and human caring.

As one who has worked as a volunteer in this field for over 25 years, establishing circles in prisons in three states and several other countries, I can attest to their power in reclaiming and restoring human beings to good lives in their communities. So many times I have been told what one of the participants says in this book: "The Circle saved my life. Without it I would be dead by now."

As the authors say, "crime isn't about broken laws but about broken lives." Human beings need human closeness. The men in our prison Circles did not have that essential support in childhood. Abandoned and neglected, they learned on the streets how to survive in isolation by cunning or aggression. Here in the Circle was their first experience of respect not earned by violence, their first experience of concern and caring by people with no ulterior motive . Time and again I have heard men declare the Circle to be the only real family they ever had, that they never understood the meaning of the word love before, but now were willing to give their lives to their new brothers. For this gift they want to give in return to help young people through the same situations. The Circle gave them their first realization of their potentials and their first real hope for their future.

In the book they write, "We treat each other in respectful and ultimately sacred ways because we see each person as part of the whole and indispensable to it. We also see ourselves as connected to all other beings, and so what happens to them affects us too. Our connectedness, gives us the responsibility to care for each other and to help mend the webs that hold us."

The premises outlined in that book of this shift are sound and necessary for this purpose, "moving from coercion to healing – from external control, "power over", exercised by the state, to "power with" people and communities, addressing causes and seeking transformation, rebuilding relationships to prevent future harms. Moving, in other words, from solely individual to individual and collective accountability: "The traditional judicial process establishes justice by imposing variations of 'getting even'....The Circle asks the victims what harm has been done as well as what can repair it and contribute to healing. Not only victims, therefore, but everyone affected is invited into the Circle's process....so that the needs surrounding crime can be addressed on many levels. The concept and practice of justice shift dramatically."

Part of the problem with the justice system is that it is basically adversarial, which often means that whoever has the means to hire the better lawyer wins. But Circles are not adversarial. This is a way we can be with each other differently without the fears and defenses that the judge-and-punish framework instills in us.

As one elder said, "How you send people away from our community is how they will come back. Send them away in anger, they come back angry; send them away with love, they come back with love in their hearts."

Perhaps the most important and encouraging effect is to urge us to become active in transforming our society, to show us the possibility of contradicting the isolation this society imposes on us and restoring real community that fosters our humanness, our creativity, and our capacity for healing one another.

I think that it is high time, in the evolution of human beings who aspire to a better world, for us to examine the moralities of punishment and war. And that will take a lot of courage, because we are all indoctrinated to a justice system and foreign policies that are immoral and restrain our growth as spiritual beings. True morality, the morality of the heart, takes a lot of courage.

So we are back to fear. Until we can transform the dominant cultures to more human ones of compassion, of caring and sharing and safety for all, we can only rely on courage. We must be brave enough to love. We must be brave enough to be honest. We must be brave enough to be generous. We must be brave enough to give-away even when we may not have enough for ourselves.

We must be brave enough to speak up for what is right, no matter what the cost. We must be brave enough to stand by people unfairly attacked and risk that attack upon ourselves. Those who go to jail to protest a war or racism or sexism or any injustice or inequality display true morality and true courage. Like that young woman who climbed a tree and lived there for a long time to keep a greedy industry from cutting it down.

I submit to you that we would all like to live in a society which truly adhered to the Golden Rule. We would like to be treated by others as they would wish us to treat them, namely with compassion and respect and actions consistent with our stated beliefs and with our caring for one another. It takes courage to maintain that integrity and that honesty in our fearful cultures. The kind of courage displayed by those who inspsire others to stand up for right against injustice. People like Thoreau, going to jail rather than pay a tax to support the war against Mexico, People like Susan B. Anthony, Margaret Stanger, Eugene Debs, Mohandas Gandhi, Dorothy Day, Martin L King, Jr., Steve Biko, Nelson Mandela. We honor the courage of those who go to war but rarely honor the greater courage of those like the Berrigan brothers who, in the name of humanity, oppose the military-industrial complex and the whole idea of warfare.

The world needs courage today. Not the false courage of armaments and the threat of violence. We need warriors that will stand up for peace. Peace has never been achieved and can never be achieved by war. It takes courage to abandon that ancient refuge and win the world over to peace. To the forsaking of arms and violence. To the destruction of all weapons of war. To a universal agreement to solve all disputes, as the Houdenosonie do, with words instead of weapons. To an insistance on closeness and openness among all people to maintain our universally desired goal: peace.

We need, in this complex world of power struggles and greed, a lot more courage to defend others than ourselves. We do not exist isolated and disconnected. We believe in love as one of our highest values, but often do not understand the bravery it takes to be truly loving in every relationship. The assault upon the earth, the water,the air, the plant and animal life, and on all the poor and hungry and homeless, the uneducated, uncared for and exploited people of the world, the elders and the children. All this affects each one of us personally, affects our children and coming generations in ways we know not.

Things to think about: we don't usually admit, even to ourselves, especially we men, the places where we become fearful. But inside yourself, can you face the place where you are afraid? The first thing to do about it is to recognize it, of couse, and then to stand up to it. Where in your life might you be able to recognize fear and just step out of it, move boldy ahead in spite of it? What relationships, what situations in your life might benefit from your just becoming fearless and boldly confronting them?

It takes courage to be yourself. To walk your talk. To live according to what you truly believe. This every one of the elders I met did.

Courage is needed at this time, perhaps more than ever. Because the blandishments of the deceptively lethal dominant culture are so insidiously seductive. Like a pretty flower that grows everywhere around us it cries out, "Eat me, I am good for you. Eat me or you will starve. I am all there is. Eat me, you will like it. I will solve your problems." But we see that it is a drug and a poison, blinding us first and then slowly killing us and all life. All our relatives. It takes real courage to turn away, to refuse this narcotic and find real life-enhancing nourishment somewhere else. It means rejecting some basic tenets of civilization and most of the ten thousand years of its lunatic history. It means returning to the Original Instructions, to the simple life of balance and harmony with Creation. To compassion and caring for all our relatives. It means returning to the circle, which offers us safety, freedom, joy and love.

Life is the Sacred Mystery singing to itself, dancing
to its drum, telling tales, improvising, playing,
and we are all that Spirit, our stories all
but one cosmic story that we are love indeed,
that perfect love in me seeks the love in you,
and if our eyes could ever meet without fear
we would recognize each other and rejoice
for love is life believing in itself.

O Humankind, we must stop fearing life,
fearing each other, we must absolutely
stop hating ourselves, resenting Creation...Life,
O Humankind, life is the only treasure.
We are the custodians of it, it is our sacred trust.
Life is wondrous, awesome and holy, a burning glory,
and its price is simply this: Courage...
we must be brave enough to love.

Hear my heart's prayer, O Humankind,
trust in love, don't be afraid. I love you
as I love life, I love myself, please
love me too, love yourself, for perfect love,
as a wise one said, casts out all fear.
If we are to live there is no other choice,
for love is life believing in itself.

                  Above all,
let us set the children free, break the traps
of fear that history has fashioned for them,
free to grow, to seek and question, to dance and sing,
to be dreamers of tomorrow's Rainbows,
and if we but give them our trust
they will guide us to a New Creation,
for love is life believing in itself.

Hear, O Humankind, the prayer of my heart.
(Excerpt from "Prayer to Humankind" - 1973)

139

12. BEAUTY

I wonder if we human beings are the only creatures who perceive Beauty. Do birds comprehend the beauty of their songs? Do dolphins have a sense of the beauty of their underwater ballet and thrilling leaps in the air? When peacocks majestically spread the fans of their tails, to peahens respond because of their beauty? What is the sense that makes a skylark rise on the wind and pour her soul in sound to the sun above and the meadow below? Besides their practical mission, do hummingbirds also relish the colors and aromas of the blossoms they enter?

I don't know if it's only anthropomorphism that makes me wonder if other species may enjoy some sort of aesthetic response beyond their pursuit of survival, of nourishment and reproduction. But it is a fact that human creatures have a strong sense of beauty. Certain arrangements of form and color, of tone and melody, of movement and posture, whether found in nature or contrived by other human beings can touch us deeply in mysterious ways, can move us suddenly to tears.

What is beauty, anyway? A question that has been the subject of much contemplation and study through the centuries. Philosophers, artists, poets substantiate the importance of this sense in our lives. From Socrates, Plato and Aristotle down to Schopenhauer and Santayana, scholars have devoted much thought to this topic. Keats' famous pronouncement that "beauty is truth, truth beauty" says more about how we may relate to existence than it explains what this aesthetic response is all about.

All the books, writings, studies, statements about beauty are interesting to consider and may send a bit of light beyond the dark edges of our consciousness, but I am not satisfied that they reach the heart of the story. What is beauty? Still it withholds its secret. It is a mystery. But it is profoundly significant somehow, an essential ingredient of our humanity.

Perhaps it can no more be defined or explained than the concepts of what is sacred, what is holy. Perhaps they are one. The beautiful and the divine. Perhaps when we are struck by a moment of beauty we are perceiving holiness. We are opened to the Spirit inherent in all Creation, and it shakes our whole being. Our carefully ordered rational explanations are short-circuited momentarily. We are adrift in mystery, opened to a glimpse of the unimaginable Source. We may feel a shiver running the nerves of our spine, creeping through our scalp, we may gasp, at times weep in an ecstasy of wonder.

The elders heard of Beauty from their elders, a concept passed from the most ancient times without much commentary. It does give us a way to refer to experiences we have had since childhood for which we have few and very inadequate words. And no preparation. Except that there is this instruction about Beauty. We are informed there is a mystery behind what we see and touch. Our elders taught us that everything has a spirit, and that this spirit is one with a Spirit that precedes and is at the heart of all Creation.

So sometimes we may have experiences that penetrate the veil, that burst past our familiar five senses to reveal an unsuspected splendor, a hidden glory behind the skin of the world. I remember lying on my back in the grass in front of the house where I was born. I was quite young, no older than four, perhaps even three. All around me was familiar, the old house and its front porch, the lilac bushes on both sides of it, the horse chestnut trees. I looked up and suddenly all of that no longer existed. I could feel the earth beneath my back, but I was all alone on it. Dark smelling soil and sweet green grass was all there was on this Earth which was bearing me upward. The earth was a platter on which I was presented to the universe. Above me was only sky. Clear and blue, the deepest blue straight above where my small body was borne.

I didn't hear any voices, no messages or explanations, and I didn't see any visions. Only the blue sky all around me. But my young mind knew I had left the Earth behind, had left all the reality I knew, and had entered into a new realm. What I felt I had no words for at the time. Looking back now I grasp for a language to convey my experience. I should create a new word for it, but how could you relate to that? It should be a word to combine our previous common references like 'power,' 'energy,' 'radiance,' 'eternity,' 'divinity,' 'splendor,' 'effulgence,' 'source,' 'provenance.' Perhaps that is what the word Beauty may convey.

I closed my eyes, thinking perhaps thereby to take it in and comprehend it, but right away that awareness departed me, and I sat up once more on the grass before my house and the lilac bushes. I had no idea what had occurred, but it made me very happy, and I kept it to myself. After eighty years the smell of lilac can still bring me that moment of rapture that I felt.

There have been quite few such revelations in my life, each one unexpected, unsought, and each one altogether different from the others. Especially strong was an hour spent in a glade within a small grove of woods in the Smoky Mountains of North Carolina. I was thirteen, and had wandered away from the group of boys studying the woods to find solitude and my own communion with nature. On entering this small enclosed glade a sudden burst of sunlight pierced the leafy canopy above and illumined area like a living presence. I stood absolutely still, my breath held, my skin brushed with a prickling, my heart drumming with unexplained excitement. A sense of (what shall I call it?) awe overwhelmed me. Again I heard no words, but I understood immediately and without doubt that I was being addressed, or allowed to see and know something not seen or known in any lesson people had given me. It could only have lasted for a few moments, but time did not exist then so eternity held me and bloomed in that light. The reason for this happening was not disclosed, and I felt no need to know it. What I felt was peace and the knowledge of a power that included and supported me. And again, joy. Then the revelation was over, and I hastened from that grove in ignorance and contentment, forever changed.

Yes, I think today I would place these emanations under the category of Beauty.

In my people's old language we have the word 'wunny'. It means 'beautiful' and it means 'happy' as well. I guess because what is beautiful makes us happy. Or what makes us happy is beautiful. When you approve of something someone does or says you can say "wuniish!' and then it means 'good!' You are saying it makes you happy. When we wish for someone's happiness we say 'may it be beautiful for you.' When people parted from each other they would say 'wuniish,' which could be translated as 'walk in Beauty.'

In the songs of the chant ways of the Dine (Navajo) there are many invocations of Beauty, as the essence of the spirit, the restoration of balance and healing, the inner rightness of Creation.

> In the house of long life, there I wander,
> In the house of happiness, there I wander,
> Beauty before me, there I wander,
> Beauty behind me, with it I wander,
> Beauty below me, with it I wander,
> Beauty above me, with it I wander
> Beauty all around me, with it I wander,
> In old age traveling, with it I wander,
> I am on the beautiful trail, with it I wander.
> (Song of Dawn Boy from the Night Chant)

> In Beauty may I dwell.
> In Beauty may I walk.
> In Beauty may my male kindred dwell.
> In Beauty may my female kindred dwell....
> In old age
> The beautiful trail
> May I walk.
> (From a Night Chant prayer)

....All things around me are restored in Beauty.
My voice is restored in Beauty.
It is finished in Beauty....
(From the Prayer of Liberation)

To my way of thinking, when I ask Creation to allow me to walk in Beauty what I'm really asking is to be able to perceive the Beauty. Because the Beauty is always there, everywhere. It is a sacred energy, a holy flame, a divinity raging hotter and more brilliant than the sun and all the stars together, pulsing within every living thing, every seed and flower and leaf, every living cell, every molecule, every atom, every proton, electron, neutron, neutrino, quark – whatever there is, and in the dance they all are doing. Most of the time I am not paying enough attention to my world to absorb the beauty that is actually there, all the time. A few times during the day it might strike me. The songs of birds just before sunrise. The whisper of the wind in the leaves of my birch and ash trees. A beckoning of blue depths in the sky, a stab of sunlight through the window, a mass of many wildflower congregations nodding over the hill, a rushing crescendo of river currents across the stones, the sighing of the tides retreating from the strand, a veil of nebulous gauze drawn from the moon that gilds the earth in magic. At these moments I am stayed in my purposefulness, and I am swallowed whole by Beauty.

"Walk in Beauty" is a wish to be aware, each moment, whatever we may be doing, that beauty is where we live. Beauty is our beginning and our end. Beauty is our source, and beauty is our goal. It is to make Beauty the purpose and meaning of our actions. Whatever we do is to make Beauty and to do it beautifully. "May Beauty surround me" means to me that I intend that my actions, the way I walk in the world, do nothing to disturb the Beauty, to upset the balance and disrupt the harmony.

I have heard elders, thinking about the old days and the old ways, speak of being warriors for Beauty. Their obligation, their instructions as they understood them, as they had been taught, was to fight for Beauty. To protect and preserve beauty. Other words elders often use are "balance" and "harmony." The world in balance is beautiful. But human beings often upset that balance. A warrior for Beauty must be devoted to restoring balance.

It was a night of the full moon on Second Mesa in Hopi Land. It was the spring of 1975. I was traveling with my new love, Emmy Rainwalker, and we had just recently decided we should come together and raise a family. We had just been visiting the elders David Monongye in Hotevilla and Thomas Banyacya in Oraibi. My truck had gotten a flat tire which delayed our leaving the mesa until the moon was high in the sky. I told Emmy that there was a voice calling to me from some distance ahead, but when we came down to the road to Winslow it was calling now from behind us. "We passed it," I said, and turned around. A little way back was a road to the right leading to the town of Shungopovi on top of the mesa, but it was too steep for my old truck. It just didn't want to haul itself and us up that incline.

"Maybe we're not supposed to go," Emmy said. I listened.

"No, it's still calling to us. I think we're supposed to walk."

It was a beautiful night to walk up that winding road in the bright moonlight. I thought we were being called to the town, whose lights we could see above. But more than half way up was a flat plateau upon which stood one of the biggest and most beautiful rocks I ever saw. I was amazed to find this great monolith, which I had not known of before, but immediately knew the voice was emanating from it.

I was now quite in awe of a spirit that might inhabit such a colossal stone, a rectangular oblong that stood on the edge of the precipice looking out over the wide desert below and blocking out hundred of stars above. We drew closer as I heard in speaking specifically to me, by only into my head so I had to report its message to Emmy as it came forth.

It told us that long ago the people had come to these mesas for refuge, guided by the spirit of Creation. Here they had lived in peace and harmony for centuries and became known as Hopi – the people of peace. Then over a hundred years ago, people of a different race and nation invaded their sanctuary and forced upon them new ways that broke the harmony and the balance, between the people and the Earth, between the people and their old ways, and making conflict among the people themselves.

Now, the voice told me, the harmony was gone, and everything was out of balance. It said that we were being called to learn and to use all our knowledge and skill in dedicating our lives to Creation.

As we turned from the stone to walk back down to the truck, we looked back once more and noticed for the first time the rock had a seam from top to bottom, right down the middle. So it was not one but two identical rocks the same size and standing together so close that no moonlight showed through the seam.

Emmy and I had two sons later, who are grown men now, and we helped build a community to raise our children together and explore how people could learn to live together in balance and harmony once more. After 35 years we are still neighbors and the best of friends. We still have the same goals and ideals, but we work in different ways now, although sometimes share in teaching a class. But for the last 25 years Ellika, my beautiful Swedish partner, and I have traveled and worked together to bring the Original Instruction to people in prison in New

England and to people in many other lands throughout the world, endeavoring to make a path of beauty that many generations can follow in safety and happiness..

To preserve harmony and to maintain balance we must have them inside ourselves. That is not always so easy in this out of balance and disharmonious culture. When we feel too much of that influence, too much tension and stress, confusion and acceleration in ourselves, it is time to separate ourselves for a while from that culture. To spend some time alone in some part of the world uninhabited and undisturbed by men. There we can slow ourselves to the pace of the natural world, quiet our minds with the sounds of the winds, and attune our spirits to the harmony of Creation all around us. The beauty that fills us there gives us strength and a paradigm for our return, a vision to hold in our quest for balance and for Beauty.

It is clear that one of our Original Instructions is to be creative. This is not an instruction I need to speak much about, except to say it is innate in us from birth, and when we are safe with our basic needs met, it will emerge in us and demand expression, and it is good for us to pay attention to these expressions, for they are sacred.

When we observe human babies as they develop, several universal human traits become quickly apparent. The first is awareness, as we see all babies fascinated and curious about everything around them. This curiosity is the main factor in the growth of human intelligence, and we see that little babies learn very quickly. The second is joy, a sense of fun and pure excitement in being alive. Little ones are forever playful and take great joy in everything, laughing easily and often as they grow. The third is love. This develops as the infant responds to the care and affection shown her and very soon she begins to display that caring and affection to others, to parents, smaller children and little animals.

The fourth trait to emerge is a result of the developing intelligence and curiosity, combined with playfulness is the instruction I mentioned – creativity. All children are naturally creative. That is inherent in all of us. Very soon the little ones begin to arrange things, to make a new thing that was not before. To mark on something with colors and find it beautiful. To make things out of sand or clay or blocks. To tell a story as they invent it, or to sing their own song. To move their bodies to the rhythms of a drum. This creativity enters into all that human beings do in which they combine thought and playfulness.

Love enters into it too, as the efforts of the little ones to make something or to perform are dedicated and given to people they love or wish to honor. Wherever I go children come to me to present pictures they have drawn and painted just for me.

The dominant culture has designated a certain type of person as an "artist" and certain vocations as "the arts." But we are all artistic. That trait may be

145

encouraged or discouraged in us as we grow, and it may develop in many ways. It is all the combining of our intelligence and our playfulness with our love and our sense of the beautiful.

So to be a human being is to be an artist, and to be an artist is to be a warrior for Beauty.

Perhaps here we should also take into account that not every artistic product conforms to our conditioned ideas. That may happen when the artist is showing us something different, expanding our awareness. Understanding that Truth is Beauty, when we are confronted by a truth that is harsh or perhaps even cruel, we at first reject it. We say, "Oh, but that is ugly!" But if it is true it fits somehow in the Creation, which is only Beauty. So for us also to fit our awareness into this existence we perhaps need that shock, that initial rejection, to feel the human reactions of horror and disgust, loathing, rage, and grief. The dark vision we have been shown and must be included in our knowledge of what is, and the cleansing of the emotions stirred by that vision, are part of our full engagement as warriors of Beauty.

Whatever ugliness we perceive has been created by the human mind, either by the conditioning of a culture, or by human activities inspired by a culture that have disturbed the harmony and made an imbalance. In the first case it is a signal to our awareness to look at the discrepancy between our culture's teachings and that of Creation. In the second it is a call to action for warriors of beauty to correct the imbalance we have made.

The true ugliness is not found in those parts of the earth where man has not intruded. There is no ugliness in death or killing that is part of the cycle of life. With our sensibilities there are those who may be disgusted and sickened by the sight of vultures or rats or maggots tearing apart a rotting and stinking carcass. But they are only doing their jobs for Creation, for balance, for Beauty. (We do not get disgusted at the thought of bacteria or other small creatures doing the same work, because we can't see them.)

What are ugly are the products of human folly. Of violence which is no part of survival but comes out of our rage, our hatred and vindictiveness, racism, sexism, ageism, and especially of our greed (oppression, exploitation, commercialism) and vanity (uniforms, medals, fashions that distort the human form). Now that's ugly!

There is a flame that burns in every human soul. A radiant power that is born in the fire of Creation and glows with a warm light that is sometimes hidden but never extinguished. This energy is everywhere, in everything, all around us and pulsing through the universe. It blazes in every blade of grass, every leaf and seed, every cell of every living thing. It throbs within each atom. So Creation is going on all the time, within us and without. This is the energy that combusts when we apply our playfulness to our intelligence with the fuel of passion from the life force within.

Perhaps that is why we hunger for Beauty in our lives. Why we are so filled with awe and wonder and joy when we perceive it. Why it brings us "thoughts that do often lie too deep for human tears." Why we need to express Beauty in our actions, in our work, and surround ourselves with it.

Traditionally we did not have vocations solely devoted to "the arts." People might specialize in making baskets or pottery or blankets or storytelling or singing, but they would also grow their corn, bake their bread, hunt and fish, make canoes and houses, and collect medicines and wild foods. The Beauty that one created in one's work, the artistry one brought to bear, was recognized and appreciated by all, but it was assumed that everyone was creative, everyone an artist in something.

People in the old days did not call attention to themselves as artists. The work itself was all that required attention, not the one who made or performed it. So people did not expect to make large amounts of money for their beadwork, or their singing, or their fancy dancing, as people do today. Things were made and done for oneself, and especially for one's people, not for fame or wealth. As a gift, perhaps to an individual or a family, or to the whole village, or to the people, for a ceremony, or a healing. There was no ego involved. Again, the first thought was for others, for the community, for the people.

There was no loss to the artist in this. The impulse of true art comes not from a need for personal recognition, but from the need to create. The concern was not for the reception of the work but for the work itself. To make it the best and most beautiful work possible.

Some arts, notably storytelling and the arts that proceed from it such as poetry and song, drama and sometimes dance, may include a further impulse to balance, to harmonize, to heal human society and relationships. This is also the result of creativity in us, the need to correct the assaults on balance and harmony made by human folly. So stories may search sometimes for the beautiful in ugliness, for the humor in stupidity, and for emotional healing and understanding through tragedy.

Such art may help us in our desires for understanding and to find order and meaning in existence. But storytelling also may exist only to show a truth, and the experience is its only meaning and purpose. Or it may exist only as Beauty itself (in the words of Archibald MacLeish: "A poem should not mean but be.")

If you think as I do that everything in Creation has an essential part to play in it, has a purpose and a reason to be there, then it makes sense for our curious minds to question. It is natural to ask the reason for our perception of Beauty, and the purpose of our need to make Beauty.

Things to think about: What are the things that are most beautiful to you? Why do you think they are beautiful? Whose standard of Beauty are you applying? Think of something that seems ugly to you. What is ugly about it? What does that mean? Who do you think is really ugly? Perhaps you might be able to change that perception – maybe you could find a hidden Beauty in that person. Is it possible you could find more Beauty and therefore more joy in your perceptions of the reality around you?

Beauty gives us pleasure. Unlike food or sex or even curiosity it seems to have no ulterior purpose beyond that. We are happy for the feeling of pleasure. But what is the purpose of pleasure? Why does Creation seem also to want us to experience joy, bliss, pleasure?

When we are pleased we are not moved to upset the balance or shatter the harmony of Creation. When we are pleased we want it to continue, we want things to be preserved. When we are pleased we are satisfied and are aware of enjoying the present moment. That is why, though there may be excitement in violence, there is no real pleasure in it. Nor in cruelty or destruction. Satisfaction can only exist in harmony, which may be stable or fluid, but is continuous.

Pleasure guides us in the way of harmony. We get pleasure in giving pleasure, so pleasure brings harmony in our relationships, with family and community, with all nature and the earth. Pleasure relaxes us, relieves our stress. But it is not necessarily relaxation. We may sometimes get pleasure in inactivity, but effort also gives us pleasure. Work is a great pleasure, and struggle can be pleasure, as in sports or the solving of problems. Pleasure changes our chemistry, makes us healthier and happier, resists diseases of stress and tension, and gives us longer life. It makes us better lovers, better parents and teachers. It exists to insure a stronger movement in evolution of the species.

Looked at in this way, it would seem that pleasure and beauty have important roles in human life. Important roles in our survival. We can appreciate why the perception of beauty and the wish to create it are built into our nature and are an important part of our Original Instructions. Just because it exists within us, because we become aware and respond to it, and because it is a profound and wonderful mystery, beauty seems to be inherent in the order of Creation and a deeply spiritual experience. The experience of Beauty sings to us from within our souls.

"Beauty is truth, truth beauty" wrote the poet Keats. Yes, and truth and Beauty are both a mystery. We devise theories of Beauty, but they do not explain why it exists; we study Creation and learn more and more about it, but we cannot explain why it exists.

From its simplest beginnings in light and energy it has grown ever more complex, from the making of elements through the making of stars through the making of life and the progress of evolution to us, the human species. It is a beautiful process, but why it should be as it is we cannot explain. There is something mysterious behind it all, which my elders and I would call the Original Instructions. They appear in the laws of physics and quantum mechanics and the processes of life that led to us, with our perception of Beauty, with our endless curiosity and search for meaning, with our delight in fun, our joy in existence, our reverence for love   And it seems that everything in Creation is connected, as my elders said, that information is passed through some medium we do not yet understand through all energy and matter, through every cell that comprises our being. We see that these cells are not all independent and isolated, but that they cooperate to combine into all the various parts of us. Those are their instructions. We human beings are not all independent and isolated beings. We are connected to all that is. And in order to become human and to be better at our becoming, we learned to cooperate also to make larger parts, which also must learn to cooperate in larger beings, as nations, as a species, part of the Earth, part of a star system, a galaxy, and other groups throughout the whole of the cosmos.

And the control system of our individual selves which we call mind has also been evolving, from the reptiles to the mammals to the humans, with our powers of language, abstraction, reasoning, logic, mathematics, and has been developing further in the center we call the heart to give preference of that system to connection, closeness, love, compassion and reverence. The story of Creation, from pure energy through the creation of matter, the stars, life, and the wonder of our complex minds whose guide is what we call "Heart" - to me this Evolution is pure Beauty. Contemplating that story inspires in me the deepest reverence for the Creation, for life, for creativity and joy, for Mystery and for Beauty.

COME HOME

We are star stuff
You and I, think of it
All billions of atoms
Bopping around our blood
In all our cells jostling, busy

Waking to another day
Regimented by DNA into bone
And nerve, skin, tooth, and hair,
Okay, folks, action, MOVE IT!
Life is calling now

And we confront each other
There you are, here am I
Star stuff each of us
We were conceived many
Billions of years ago

In the roaring factory
Of some churning sun
That gasped, died, and hurled
All that hydrogen, oxygen
Carbon and other refuse

Spinning into waiting space
Collecting on this welcoming rock
As water, stone, and many tiny
Squiggly things connecting
Feeding, growing, changing

Evolving to us – here we are
Ancestral star voices in us
Calling out to each other
In deep longing, here I am
Come home, come home

EPILOGUE

My gratitude to all the dear and generous elders I attended forty years ago has no limit. Although distinctly different from each other, they shared qualities that impressed my searching mind deeply. The qualities I have tried, not well enough, I fear, to emulate in myself and describe in these pages. The qualities of respect, gratitude, and awareness they exhibited at every moment. Honesty of course, but always with humor. Hospitality, generosity, humility and patience – these were just part of their natures. Courage one might only note in considering the dedication of their whole lives to their beliefs under the greatest difficulties and opposition. These people I revered were not uniformly honored in their own communities, and I know the indifference and occasional opposition of other native people to their actions and teachings was difficult for them, but they never let on and I never heard them say a negative word about anyone. Their love for me gave me the confidence to walk in a good way, and the memory of that love still lifts me up when my heart is brought low by disappointments. They kept steadfastly to the good red road and wherever they walked they walked in Beauty.

Dear Reader, you are a member now of our small circle, in the larger circle of over six billion people in the world only a very few are readers. And of those who do read books, only a very few will have the interest to read a book of this kind. So you are a small and select group. Consider that you have made a journey to here, to listen to many elders through me. I would like more than anything to show you the kindness and the love which they showed to me. I would wish that their words and their being might transform your life as they did mine.

For then I could say to you, as they said to me, walk this good red road in a sacred manner, let your lives be a teaching, and go when invited and speak when asked of the Original Instructions to be a true human being, and my blessings and the blessing of the elders will be with you always.

There have been lately a number of gatherings of elders from many indigenous people around the world. Another book you would like is called <u>Grandmothers Counsel the World</u>, in which many grandmothers speak of their concerns today. They all assert the clear hope that such circles will spread, and when they have covered the world it will return to the way of Creation's instructions.

Very recently a large number of elders gathered on land not far from my home. which friends of mine have dedicated to the Earth, to peace and respect for all life. These elders had come from many of the First Nations all across Turtle

151

Island. I was attending a meeting of the European Social Forum at the time and could not be there, but my brother reported to me about it. It seemed it was a very wonderful and powerful gathering, elders spontaneously feeling the need to meet and share their insights about the most urgent message for the world today. What was remarkable was that they had each one come to the same conclusion. Now is the time, they said, to stop all our attention to our differences, and to come together as one people, one family, the children of Mother Earth. Our mother is being threatened, and we must all come together in her defense before it is too late. We must give up all our hatred our anger, our suspicion of each other, our attacking and badmouthing each other. Our mother weeps that her children are still fighting. She wants us to be happy, to be at peace, and to provide a healthy, safe, and happy life for all our children.

It brought me so much joy to know that the other elders are coming together, that we all agree. Together we must keep working to turn this society around, to wake the people to the damage that has been done by following the ways of commercialism materialism, power and domination. To return to the way of Creation, the Original Instructions, such as Respect, the Circle, and Thanksgiving.

There are also other instructions that are part of the life and teaching of all the elders past and present. I did not include a chapter for each of them because they are woven into all the chapters and into our basic human nature. They are the instructions of harmony, balance, cooperation, caring and love.

I have tried as best I could in my life to serve my elders wishes and bring their teachings to any who sought them, and I offer this book as a stumbling attempt at that. The elders showed so much love to me, and in their whole lives, that you may wonder why I did not devote one of these chapters to the instruction of love. It is at the center of our being, after all. We believe in love, extol it, search for it, sing about it, write about it, and preach it in our religions and philosophies (with a caution not to confuse it with desire). I did not write so much of love here because most people already realize that it is our very essence. Our problem is in locating, distinguishing, and living it. That, I feel, is best approached through the first instruction of Respect.

All that is needed, beyond respect, is closeness. Because if in respect we keep our distance, deep love will not flourish. Love comes with understanding, and understanding comes with respect and closeness.

The Buddha taught the primary virtues of wisdom and compassion. I believe compassion is the natural outgrowth of wisdom, and vice-versa.

Jesus taught that the only principles we need are to love God and our neighbor. Perhaps today we need to re-define the concept of God and neighbor for our own time.

Not everyone believes in what other people call God. I think, as I said in my first book, that fact need not separate us from each other. If you believe there is an intelligence or spirit that designed and issued forth this Creation with a purpose, then your work, I submit, is to find this design and purpose and align and harmonize yourself with it; and if you believe there is no pre-ordained design or purpose, then your work is to create one that works for you, and in working for you it must of course work for all. I believe they amount to the same work. I believe that wisdom will show that respect guides us to the same place, driven by the same engine: the engine of love.

So. Love God? Okay, but if you don't like that word, love Life, love Existence, love the Earth.

And your neighbor? Your neighbor is not just the human being next to you, it is the grass, the trees, the flowers and fruits, the other creatures that crawl and run and swim and fly, and all the human ones in every land and culture, as well as the winds and the waters, and even your relatives in the distant heavens.

At the time when I am transcribing these thoughts, early in the 21st century, it seems to me there are two imperatives for the human species that must supersede all other goals now for every one of us. The first and foremost is to save this planet for life, to stop the destruction of the Earth and make it safe and healthy for all life.

Most of the human beings alive right now have no idea how urgent and necessary that is. We are making the only home we can have unfit for human habitation. We can see that today in all the problems we have of health and safety and quality of life, and it will get worse unless we all stop what we are doing, how we are living, make sacrifices and take drastic steps to redress the damages we have already done.

I think our job now has to be to make friends with everybody so we can pull together in this huge work. Which means that the second imperative is to end war and resolve our conflicts peaceably. As the Great Law of Peace says, with words not weapons. We are fighting with each other while our house is burning down.

So love. Yes. Of course. Love god means love the Earth, love Life. Love your neighbor means love all your relatives, the whole great web of Creation.

Love is the center, and it is the activity of Creation, the center of our being and the circle of existence. Truly it makes the world go round.

The elders tell us this: our nations are not our primary concern. Your family is your primary concern. And we are all family. Our children are our primary concern, and our grandchildren and all the unborn that descend from us.

We must tell our children how it was
How the people helped each other
That no one should be cold or hungry
For the young were loved and fondled
And the old respected and cared for
And honor was given to all the spirits
To the ones who had gone and the yet unborn
And throughout the universe
All things were touched with beauty

   *   *   *

It is time to free ourselves
It is time for us all to go home
Home to our families and our villages
And walk again the ancient Path of Beauty

Now the Turquoise Woman has begun
To wash the horizon with her hue
Leaving only the Morning Star and
The slender silver horn of the New Moon
Soon the Seneca Chief will come
And burn tobacco for the new day
And I will pray for this rebirth of light.

O You who bring the day
Thank you for the Sun again
For another chance to learn
Thank you for this life
And all my relatives
Throughout the universe
Known and unknown

*　　　*　　　*

Thank you for my mind that knows beauty
And my heart that knows the abundance of love
And thank you for letting me live to see
This return of the spirit of our people

(Excerpts from "Night Watch by the Sacred Fire"-1974)

I encourage your contacting us and connecting in any way to work on making
a better world for our children and the generations to come.

Wuniish – May it be beautiful for you.

Other Books

...In *Return to Creation* he uses his storytelling talents to take us back to the home of his ancestors in southern New England in order to bring us an awareness of natural law, known as the Original Instructions to indigenous peoples all over the world.

....Guided by a vision, Medicine Story shares the ancient knowledge to benefit not only his native people, but all people in the belief that the tribal way of life may be the only way left to save humanity.

...Much of this book is written in the wonderfully poetic manner I find so moving in Native storytelling, but it is far from being overly idealistic. It is, more often, a practical guide - a handbook for parents and community leaders alike. Medicine Story is an admirable man, an elder most worthy of respect and honor, and an author of great talent. His wisdom and sincerity are undeniable. *Return to Creation* is a book worth reading."

-Odyssey

The appeal of this book is its lyrical simplicity. It can be recommended to those seeking a broader understanding of how modern Americans of Indian heritage are attempting to preserve their views of human nature and increase understanding about the place of humankind in the greater cosmos of which we are all ultimately a part - less important than we might think but perhaps of greater value than we imagine."

- **The New Press**, Spokane, WA

In *Return to Creation*, Medicine Story gives the reader a reserved, front-row seat at his council fire. These are the stories you might have heard if you had been following Medicine Story around the country for the past 20 years absorbing his teachings....There is plenty of cosmology and spiritual theory here, for those who are interested. But there are also more "practical" sections on subjects such as child-rearing, honoring elders, and the ways of men and women.

Convergence, Concord, N.H.

...I have decided that your book is what I am giving to most family and friends for Christmas this year, and so I decided I will call every book store in the greater Portland area and ask them to order it so that they will become aware of it, and I will rave about how wonderful it is so much that they will become curious and order more...

I need to get another copy of your book for me as a loaner copy, to help me promote your book, as I am unwilling to loan our copy that you signed. I don't have many precious material possessions, but this is one of them.

-Pam Leo, **The Family Business**, Gorham, ME

I would like to thank Medicine Story for his sharing this superb book of knowledge and story; because there are so many people who are not sure what is going on in the mind, body, and spirit of things. This book will enlighten and connect you with the self, others, earth and sky ...enjoy -**Windsong Alden Blake, Chief, Assonet Wampanoag**

"Thank you, Medicine Story, for sharing our traditional values with the world." **-Drifting Goose, Supreme Sachem of the Wampanoag Nation**

"A valuable contribution to public understanding of our culture." – **Dr. Helen Attaquin, Wampanoag**

Enclosed is a copy of my Boston Herald column containing mention of *Return to Creation*. It is a thoughtful, superlatively written book that makes a lot of sense. I hope I've stimulated my readers to go pick up a copy. I wish you the best in all your endeavors, Sincerely, Judy Bass

A NATIVE AMERICAN FORESEES BETTER WORLD

There probably isn't a perfect remedy for modern society's ominous problems, but one newly released book does present many viable ideas for positive change. – *Return to Creation*, by Medicine Story.

Based in New Hampshire, the author is a Wampanoag elder, storyteller, lecturer and spiritual leader. In "Return to Creation", he adopts an optimistic, gentle tone to suggest that tribal ways dating back thousands of years can be used today to achieve widespread harmony and stability.

Medicine Story emphasizes mutual trust and respect, along with the interconnectedness and sanctity of all living things. People are gradually emerging from their self-absorption, he said in a phone interview, and rediscovering the value of "helping the planet, helping people, helping society, and finding something worthwhile to do." -Judy Bass, The Boston Herald Sept 29, 1991

My name is Kimberley Paterson and I am a writer and journalist in Auckland, New Zealand. I've just found an email address for you. I wanted to write and thank you for your work.

I read your book many years ago and, when editing a magazine Rainbow News printed a couple of quotes from it. I think I most love your piece `Movement' ... It is time for us to go beyond where we have been...

I have read that piece out to groups many times ... when I've left workplaces, when I've been asked to speak to groups and again, will do this Sunday when asked to address a spiritual fair, New Spirit festival, in Auckland.

I wanted you to know what a profound influence your words and attitude has had on my life and thank you from the other side of the world

I recently read RETURN TO CREATION and I was so touched and moved I wanted to write and tell you: thank you for making this world a better place and thank you for giving the rest of us hope, encouragement and inspiration. I have read a lot of books in my life. I can honestly say I have never been so moved by someone's words before. Not only did I feel you were speaking directly to my heart, but it was as if you took everything I have long suspected and said, "Yes! Your suspicions are correct!....." I hope people like you will continue to speak your heart....there are a lot of us out here who would like to start over again, who would like to learn, who care as much as you do about the earth, the future, what is right and natural, about what is sacred and holy. - Laurie Baardse

I want to express my gratitude that there are still people like you and other Indians around fighting for the cause of sanity and for the cause of saving nature and the human spirit. You, Manitonquat, are just a human being yourself and I know you haven't all the answers to humanity's many ills. But you are a man of authority in some way, under the guidance of the Great Spirit. I can feel this in the way you write. And I thank the Great Spirit for books written by men like you. I believe personally that the American Indian has very much to contribute in these times of crisis for the whole world. Things that I have read by members of your people have always strengthened me and brought me back closer in touch with my spirit/ _ Richard Waring, Quebec, PQ

With all my heart I would like to thank you for your book Return to Creation which has a great influence on my thoughts. A year ago I had the pleasure of listening to your stories in Sandviken, (Sweden)...Afterwards I bought the book from your publisher and I'm now reading it for the second time. And it's getting even stronger. There is a growing interest here in Sweden, and I hope it isn't temporary. Classe Waltin

"Your book, Return to Creation, has been like a cool breeze in the hot stillness of a summer day. The message heralds the harvest that comes from the heat of summer...Before I read your words I had little understanding of my own outrage and frustration with a society that seemed to purposefully restrict and war against the innocent beauty and wisdom of its youngest members...Thank you for your book." – Dee Calley

159

Thank you for the book <u>Return to Creation</u> - it is an excellent work! Very thought-provoking - especially regarding community, treatment of women, and raising children. It is a must-read for anyone contemplating marriage and family. I am grateful to have such a guide. Thank you most sincerely - Mark Wilson

I thank you for your work that is so important for me and everyone else.... Words can never explain what that means to me. Thank you for giving me reasons to go on living, working and loving. Thank you for making me feel something worth and important and thank you for showing me that IT IS POSSIBLE to make the world a little better if I go on trying and working like you do. You open hearts and show that in the inside of all of us there's the beauty of the whole world.... You gave me back the real worth of every touch and smile and laugh that I can get.... Thank you for your great work! You're giving so much hope to me! - Eva Peters, Schöneck, Germany

I had almost lost my hope one morning when I came across your book in a shelf at this eco-community called Gaija here in Finland, it was from one of your visits in Finland from 1999(Return to Creation). The book popped out of the shelf into my eyes and I read it at once. I have to say that I went from tears of sadness and neglect to tears of hope and joy in the process of reading your book. It really helped to find your thoughts so near mine, even though we share no immediate cultural background...you gave me new hope on my way and I now know that what I'm doing is right. I learned new courage from your thoughts and feel proud of my works of creativity again. Thank you for your words. - Jan "Anguvard" Jämsén, Finland

CHANGING THE WORLD

I spoke to a group of high school students about "Changing the World" and they all got excited and told me they wanted to change the world too. So I had a weekly circle with them in which we looked at what is wrong with the world and thought about how we would want it to be. At the end of the school year I wrote my most recent book and called it <u>Changing the World.</u> I will include a short selection from it here at the end.

Whenever I write I have a specific reason and purpose for that piece of writing. My life is so full of meaningful and gratifying activity it requires a great determination to wring any time for writing from it. I always wonder from which area I should steal some hours: from our work in the prisons, from answering calls for teaching or for counseling, from organizing international family summer camps, or from building a global network to re-create society for our highest human aspirations of peace and justice.

Also, when I consider all the millions of books in the world and the thousands that are produced every year, it is extremely daunting., How can I have the effrontery to cover yet more hundreds of clean pure white pages with yet more verbiage?

So you may be sure I do not embark on the task of writing any book and nor do I offer it lightly and frivolously. I really have other very important things to do with this precious time. And so do you.

My first book, <u>Return to Creation</u>, took me twelve years to complete, stealing a little time from my life here and there. I wrote it because for years I had been following the instructions of my visions and my elders to bring the traditional wisdom of our old ways to whomever would ask for them. As I was getting mail from distant places and more people than I could visit in person, I wrote the book. After two decades I still get letters from all over the world, from people I will never meet, thanking me for that book which helped to change their lives in positive ways. Once I returned from an extended speaking tour abroad to find a Japanese man who had read the book (in Japanese it is called <u>The Love of an Indian</u>) and immediately got on a plane, speaking only a few words of English, and flew to meet me!

My next book, <u>Children of the Morning Light</u>, I wrote to preserve the creation stories of the Wampanoag as my grandfather imparted them to me from oral tradition for our own people and other children of the future.

Then I felt the need to describe in detail our program in the prisons of New England for Native men and other interested seekers. The program has been such a resounding success that I wanted everyone around the world to know of it and use our experience for their own programs. I also wanted to put forth my vision for an ex-prisoner, ex-addict center somewhere in the country, in a natural setting, run by the ex-convicts themselves in the spirit of the circle. This small book, Ending Violent Crime, has been available everywhere free for downloading from the Internet.

Another book, The Circle Way, was written at the request of a number of circles I had inspired which wanted more guidelines and suggestions for creating and nurturing circles. On my seventy-fifth birthday I brought out a little story for children, Granddaughter of the Moon, which I also illustrated. Three years ago I wrote a book called Changing the World, a vision of the future developed through a class by that name that I taught for a year at a Waldorf High School.

Just recently I have published Wampanoag Morning, a book of stories about life in our area just before the invasion of the Europeans, and Grandfather Speaks, a small book of verse.

Still in the writing stages are Have You Lost Your Tribe? A book about communities and the ecovillage movement, and The Circle and the Pyramid, a history of humankind from the perspective of a tribal person. Still in the planning stage is Tear Down the Walls, a book about justice and punishment, my thoughts after twenty four years of work in the prison systems and thirty five years teaching childraising to parents. I look forward to completing more books of poetry and stories, and perhaps a sequence of novels.

An Excerpt from <u>Changing the World</u>

Broad studies of human societies show us that they are most human, most considerate and beneficial to all, when they are egalitarian, when deliberation and decision-making are distributed most equally. When power becomes concentrated in an individual or a special group oppression and injustice appear and grow.

As Lord Acton observed, power corrupts, and only the true equality of small groups, where there is time and care for each person to be heard, can protect our communities from that corruption. From the beginning civilized societies were corrupt, for instance, by the exclusion of the female half of the population, power resting only in the male, further narrowed to the warrior and the wealthy. The system of what is called checks and balances has failed to address this unequal distribution of power to the wealthy.

True democracy does not exist in any of the nations of the world, because of size and the influence of wealth. But it has existed in those tribal societies where each person has an equal voice, where communities are small enough for people to know and hear each one.

Is it possible for a planet of more than six billion people to have economic, political, cultural and spiritual organization based on units small enough to secure such a true democracy, maintaining equality and the common values of each community, yet cooperating in larger projects and organization for a greater good globally?

As a tribal person who has experienced living in a variety of tribal communities and who has studied the evolution of human society, I have come to the conclusion that it is possible for humanity to achieve a society that is truly egalitarian and enhances the creativity, contentment, closeness and love of every member. I see indications of that in all the work I have done with circles and communities for the past forty years.

What follows is my own personal conception and vision of how that might be achieved. I offer it as part of our common search to make our lives, the lives of the coming generations, and that of the Earth and our fellow creature species, better, healthier, safer and happier.

I have chosen to present this vision in a compact version, as a visit to a village of the future. It is a seed I hope may find fertile ground in your heart and mind to grow into your own vision, to share and keep us moving forward together.

I intend to begin to nurture this seed with others as soon as we may find a spot to begin our first Circle Way Village. It will not develop just like this vision, because it will be the product of all the different people who build it. But I believe the basic human principles behind it are ones to which most will find agreement.

Further articles from my newsletter, our schedule photos from our camps, and links to worthy sites, can all be found on our web site www.circleway.org

About The Author

Manitonquat (Medicine Story) is an elder, storyteller, and retired ceremonial leader of the Assonet Wampanoag. A former editor of the native liberation journal *Heritage* and poetry editor of *Akwesasne Notes*, he is the author of eight subsequent books.

He was a co-founder of the Tribal Healing Council, a member of the North American Indian Spiritual Unity Movement, directs the Mettanokit Prison Circle programs in Massachusetts and New Hampshire, is advisor to the Nature School. A counselor and teacher of counseling, he lectures widely on justice, peace, the environment, conscious evolution and creating a truly human society. He delivered the keynote speech at a United Nations gathering on non-violence honoring Mahatma Gandhi.

Together with his wife, the Swedish actress and playwright Ellika Lindén, Manitonquat creates international family camps in many countries to give the experience of tribal living, working, playing, sharing everything and taking care of the children and elders together. Their dream is to create an international Circle Way Village where human beings may safely raise their children together in peace, freedom, equality, cooperation, and love, caring for each other and our relatives that share this beautiful Mother Earth, thus fulfilling our Original Instructions.

His newsletter *Talking Stick* can be found on the Internet at *circleway.org*.

About The Author

CPSIA information can be obtained
at www.ICGtesting.com
Printed in the USA
LVHW032200050122
707898LV00006B/538